AF225796

THE 54 - AND THEN SOME

MIMI SCHLICHTER

THE 54 - AND THEN SOME

The 54 Falmouth Beach Paintings in 54 Days Project, expanded edition with The Other 46

Mimi's Art

Other books by Mimi:

The 54: 54 Falmouth Beach Paintings in 54 Days - paperback, 78 pages (2021) ISBN 978-0996330848

The 10 Things: An Invitation to Dive In - paperback, 44 pages (2017) ISBN 978-0996330824

The 54 and Then Some:
The 54 Falmouth Beach Paintings in 54 Days Project,
expanded edition with The Other 46

First Printing, 2021

For permission requests,
please contact the author.
MimisArt.com

Artist photo by Vagabond View Photography
Cover design by Mimi Schlichter

Schlichter, Mimi
The 54 and Then Some:
The 54 Falmouth Beach Paintings in 54 Days Project,
expanded edition with The Other 46
Copyright ISBN 978-0-9963308-5-5

This book is dedicated
to all who love Falmouth
and its beaches.

What began as a self-imposed discipline
took on a life of its own.

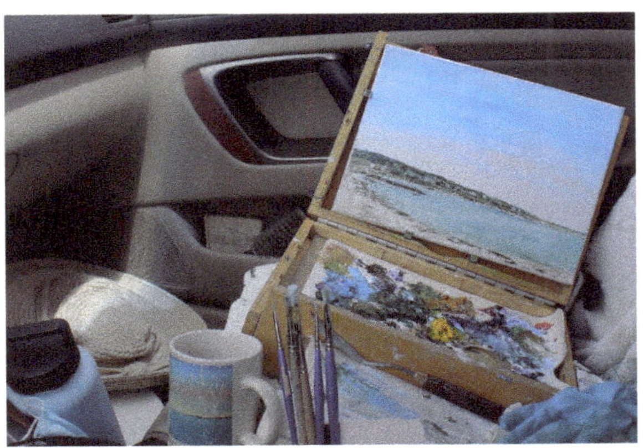

CONTENTS

CONTENTS

CONTENTS

CONTENTS

CONTENTS

CONTENTS

CONTENTS

CONTENTS

THE PROJECT

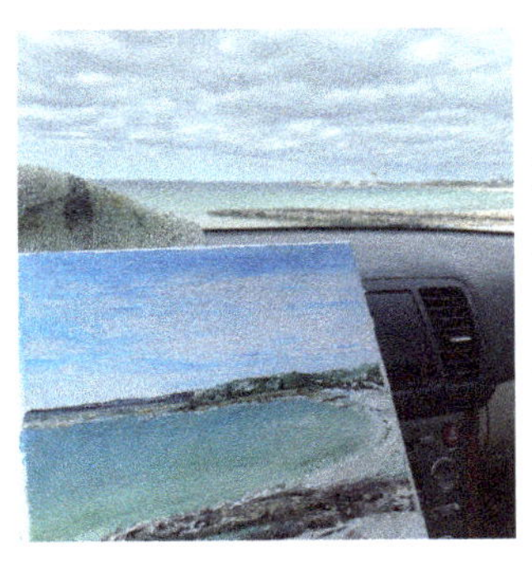

On April 1, 2020 the Town of Falmouth closed its beach parking lots as a proactive measure to reduce Covid 19 viral spread. They remained closed 54 days.

With their closing, I lost the option of painting beach scenes from the front seat of my car, as I often did.

Fast forward one year.

On a day in late March, 2021, I found myself sitting in my car in the parking lot at Chapoquoit Beach, painting, and wondering *why didn't I do this more often last year?"*

Then I remembered.

I couldn't get there.

The idea came to me to celebrate how life is different this year. I went home and looked up the dates of the closing. April 1 through May 24.

So on April 1, 2021, I began a series of 54 paintings of the Falmouth beaches. My goal was to complete the paintings in 54 days, one a day, every day, by May 24. It was not a challenge. It was a project. I simply made the commitment to paint. That's all.

Each day, I posted the new painting of the day on a Facebook group page called "Fabulous Falmouth." I had no idea the project would gather the following it did. I was humbled. Inspired. And propelled forward to complete the project. I owe a huge debt of gratitude to every single person who liked, loved, or commented during the 54 days.

THE PROCESS

All paintings were completed in a style and process known as *alla prima.*

What does that mean?

In Italian, *"alla prima"* means *"at first attempt."* In other words, the paintings were completed in a single session, on location, without further refinement in the studio.

I painted predominantly with palette knife. At times quick, decisive strokes. Other times rendered lovingly, as smooth innuendo of movement, a caress of the knife through the paint across the canvas. Do something 54 days in a row, and it does get easier. One learns along the way. Both what to do, and what not to do.

All are oil paintings, completed mostly with a palette knife, one with traditional brushes, and a few with a combination of both.

Original sizes varied, including: 4" x 12", 5" x 7", 6" x 6", 8" x 8", 8" x 10" and 9" x 12." This will account for the variance in sizes of the images within the following pages.

Though most of the original paintings have already found new homes, the collection is available as fine art prints. There is a QR code link to my website at the back of this book should you like to know more details about the prints.

THE BOOK

Create 54 new paintings in 54 days and it seems only logical to put together a show.

Logical unless two thirds of the paintings sold during those 54 days.

So there will not be a show in the traditional sense of paintings on the wall.

Rather, I present to you this book, a little art show of your own that you may revisit any time you'd like. I present the paintings in chronological order, instead of grouped by beach, so you may walk through the progression of the 54 days. Comments from me are brief, mostly from the original social media posts. You may also view the paintings on my website via the QR code at the back of the book.

I invite you to sit, quietly, with the images, because I believe it is far more important to ask what you, the viewer, see, rather than what I, the artist, saw. Allow them to speak to you. Or simply enjoy the colors. Maybe even take time to consider the following questions.

- *What do you feel when you look at the image?*
- *Have you been there before?*
- *Might you like to go there now, at least in your mind?*

May the paintings in the following pages invoke joy, peace, and smiles. Thank you for taking the time to look.

The project includes only those beaches listed on the Town of Falmouth's website.

Bristol - days 2, 18, 27, 36, 45

Chapoquoit - days 1, 12, 20, 23, 29, 31, 33, 39, 46, 49, 54 *(closest to my home!)*

Falmouth Heights - days 6, 14, 25, 34, 42

Grew's Pond, Goodwill Park - days 10, 37

Megansett - days 5, 11, 22, 26, 47, 50, 53

Menauhant - days 9, 13, 30, 40

Old Silver - days 7, 15, 21, 32, 48

Stoney/MBL - days 3, 16, 24, 38, 41

Surf Drive - days 4, 17, 23, 35, 37, 43, 52

Woodneck - days 8, 19, 28, 44, 51

DAY 1, APRIL 1 - CHAPOQUOIT BEACH

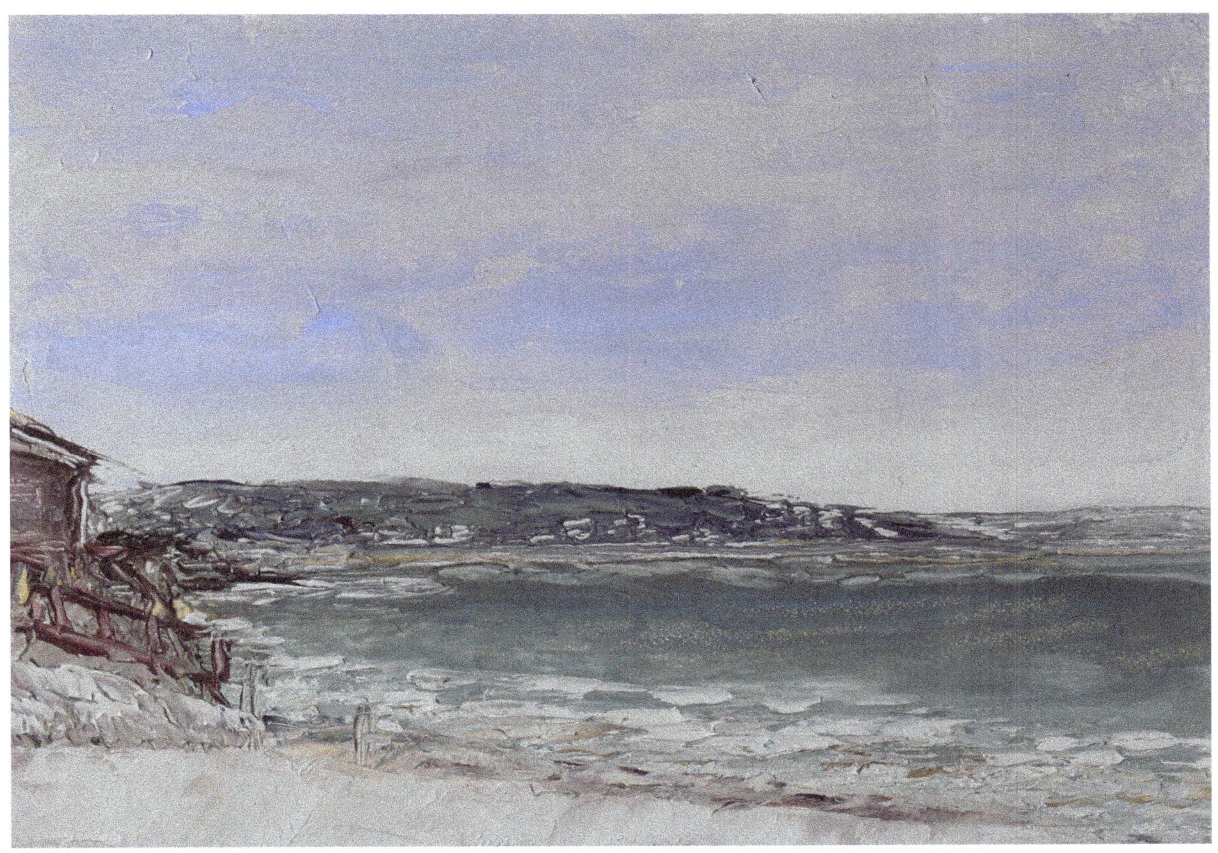

The project begins at Chapoquoit Beach, in spite of the dreary skies. This is the only painting that includes a building structure. I tend to leave those out, focusing on sky, land, and water.

DAY 2, APRIL 2 - BRISTOL BEACH

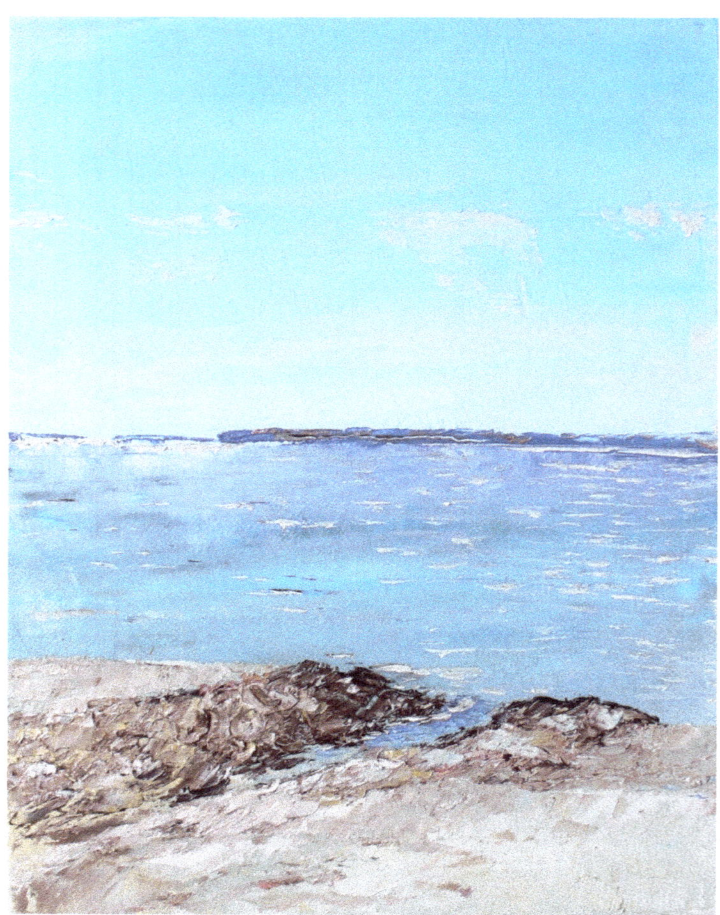

Bright sun today!!!

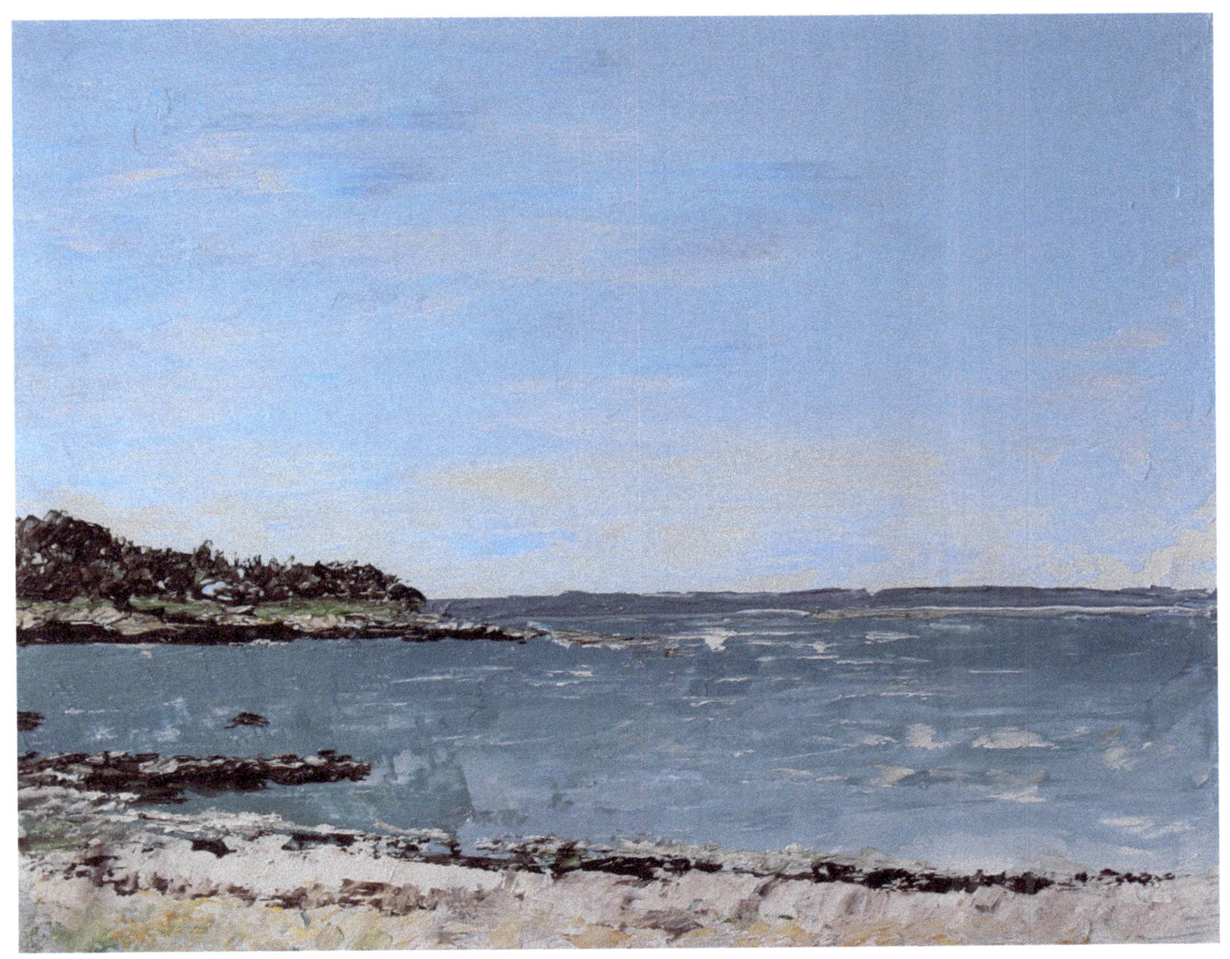

Spectacular day!

DAY 4, APRIL 4 - SURF DRIVE BEACH

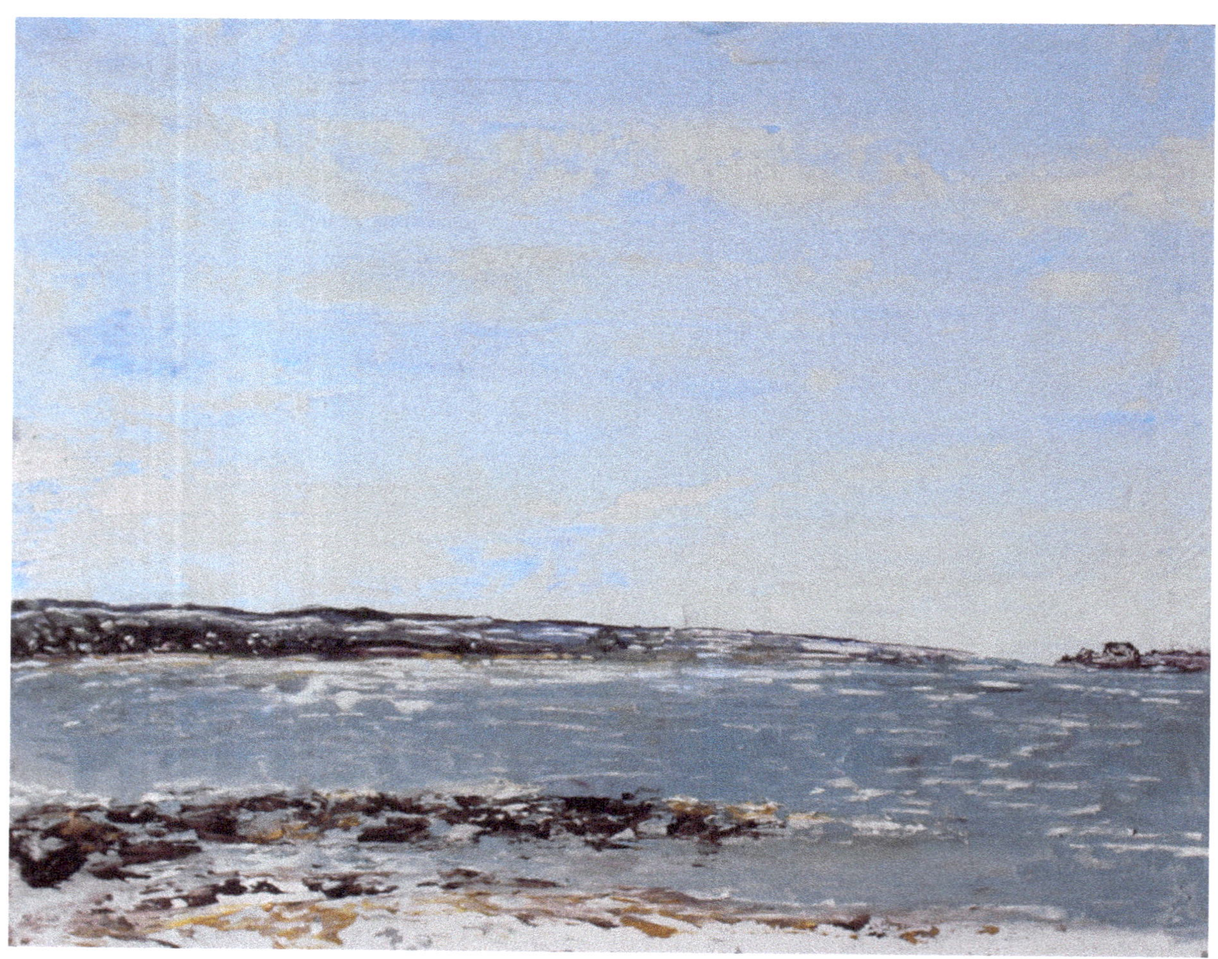

Do you see Nobska lighthouse in the distance on the far right side of the painting?

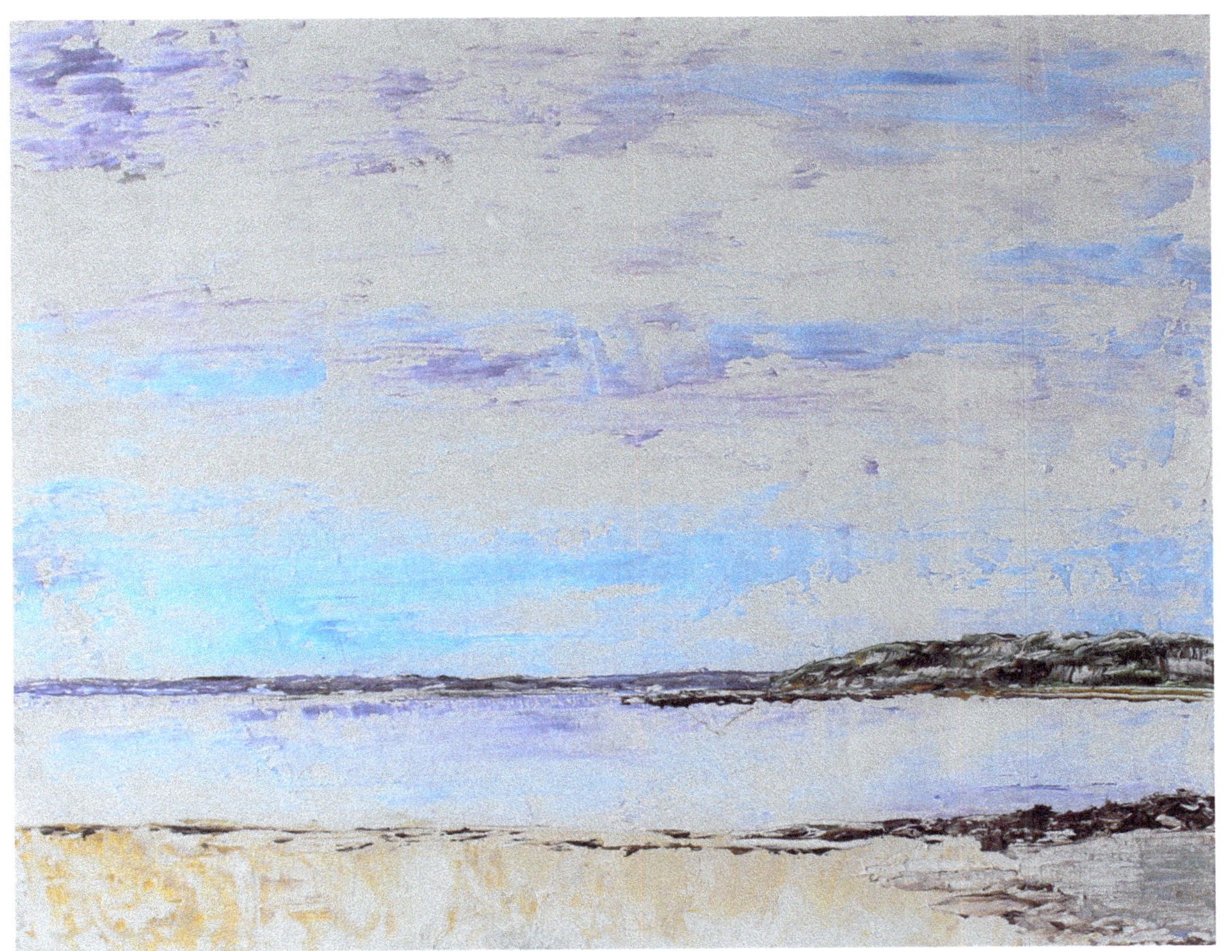

I headed out with the intention of going to Old Silver Beach but my car wanted to go to Megansett Beach, so Megansett it was! Two seagulls hanging out quite close to the car. Pretty sure they were hoping for food. In spite of what Mary Poppins said, DO NOT FEED THESE BIRDS! Two will turn into twenty five in about ten seconds. I think they lurk in the dunes.

DAY 6 , APRIL 6 - FALMOUTH HEIGHTS BEACH

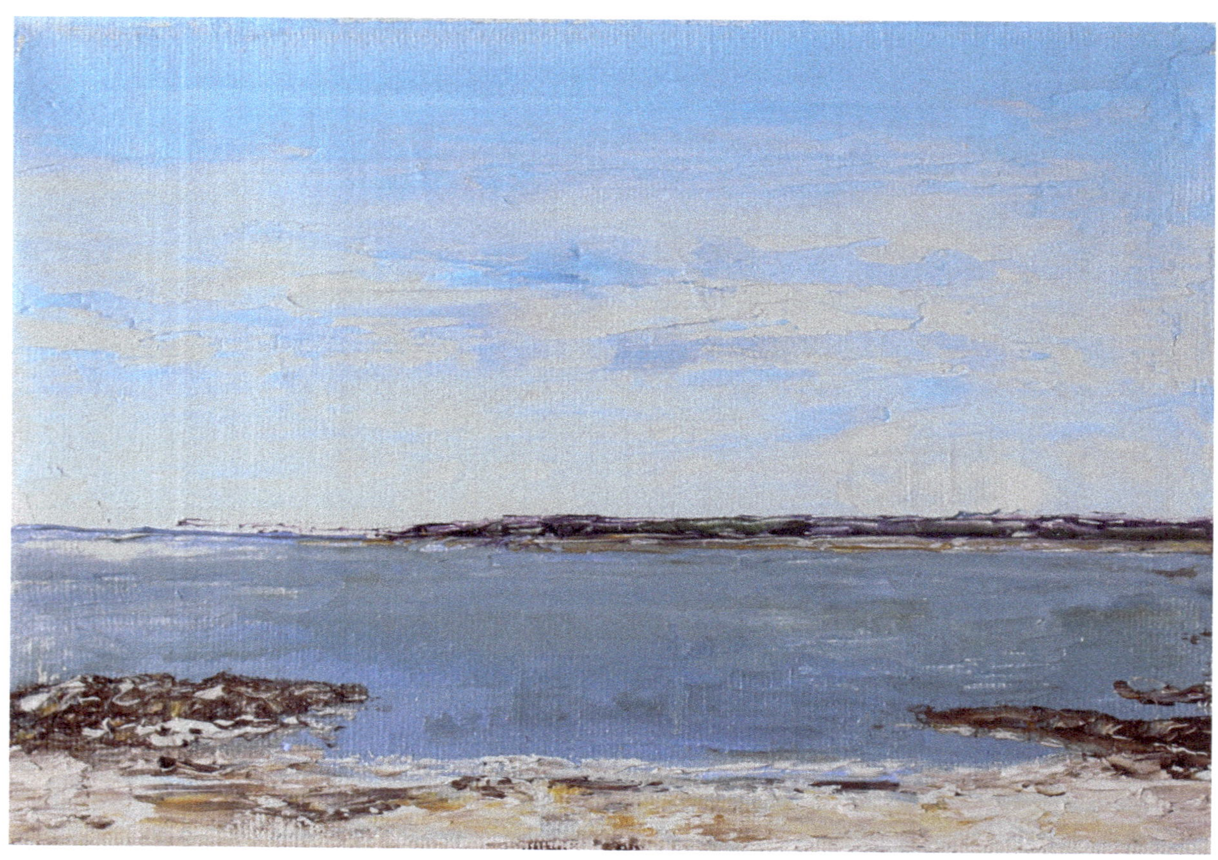

The beach at Falmouth Heights might really be considered to be about Martha's Vineyard, as it is the dominant view!

DAY 6, APRIL 6 - FALMOUTH HEIGHTS BEACH

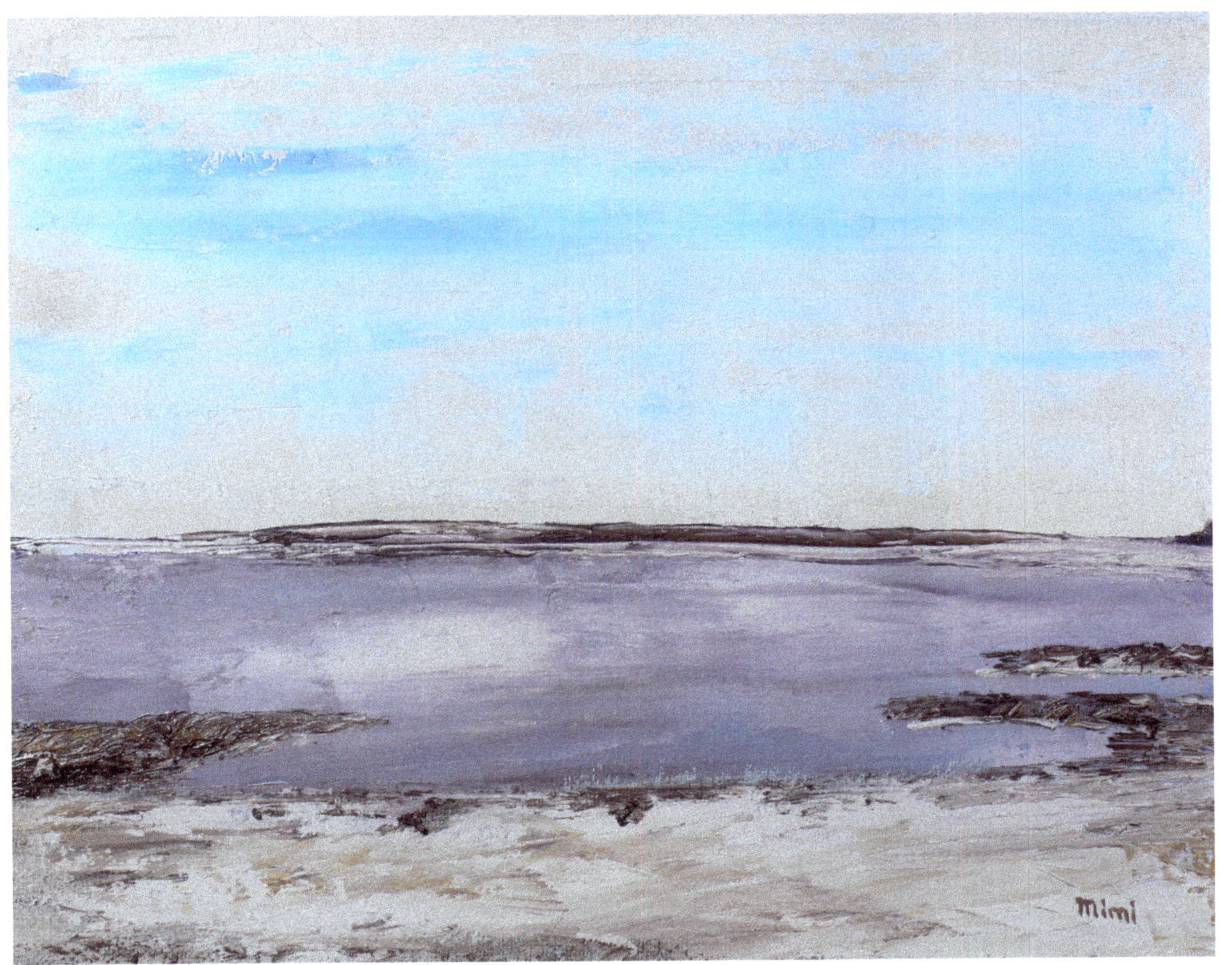

Yes, I am aware. I already posted one for Day 6. Painted a second one, also at Falmouth Heights Beach. If I made the rules for the project, I get to break them, don't I?

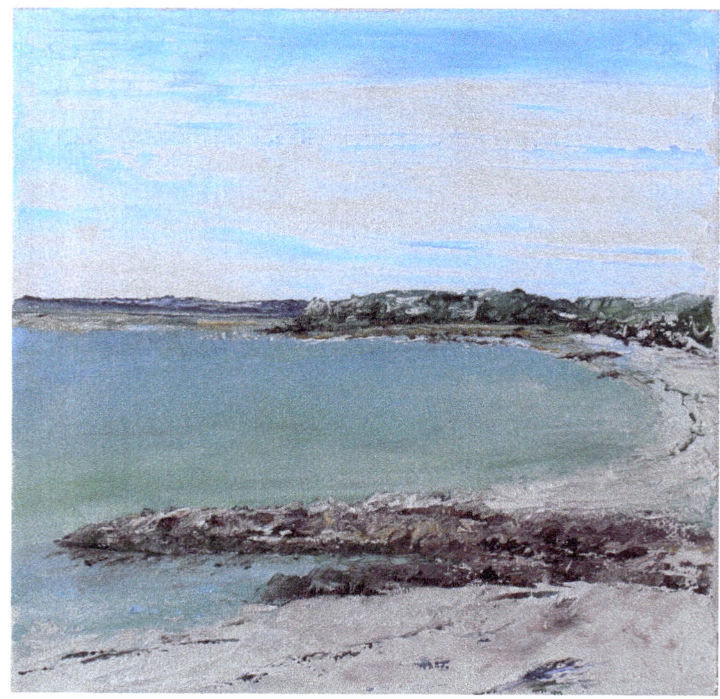

Social media post for this day said, "This is how the magic happens" since I posted a time lapse video of me painting. You may view it on Youtube by scanning the QR code on page 66.

DAY 8, APRIL 8 - WOODNECK BEACH

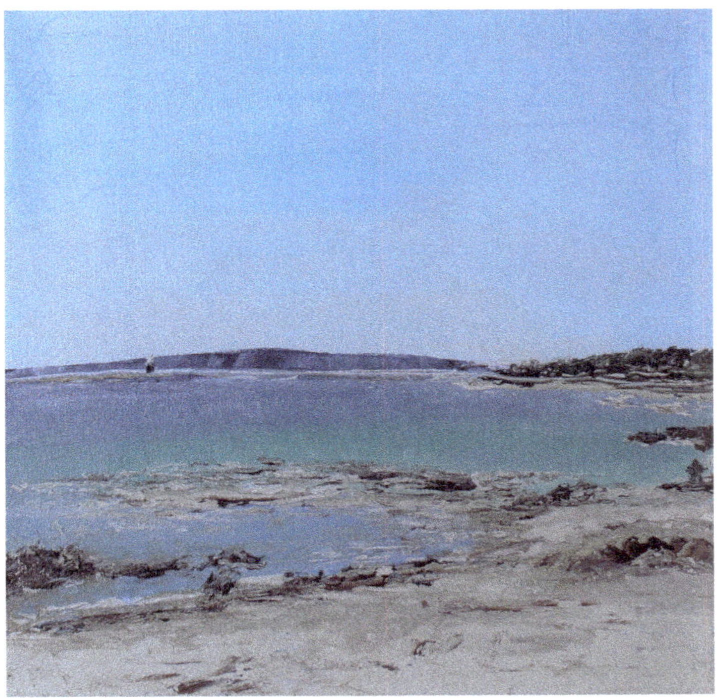

No beach view from this parking lot so out of the car and onto the sand. Scan the QR code on page 66 to watch a video filmed on site.

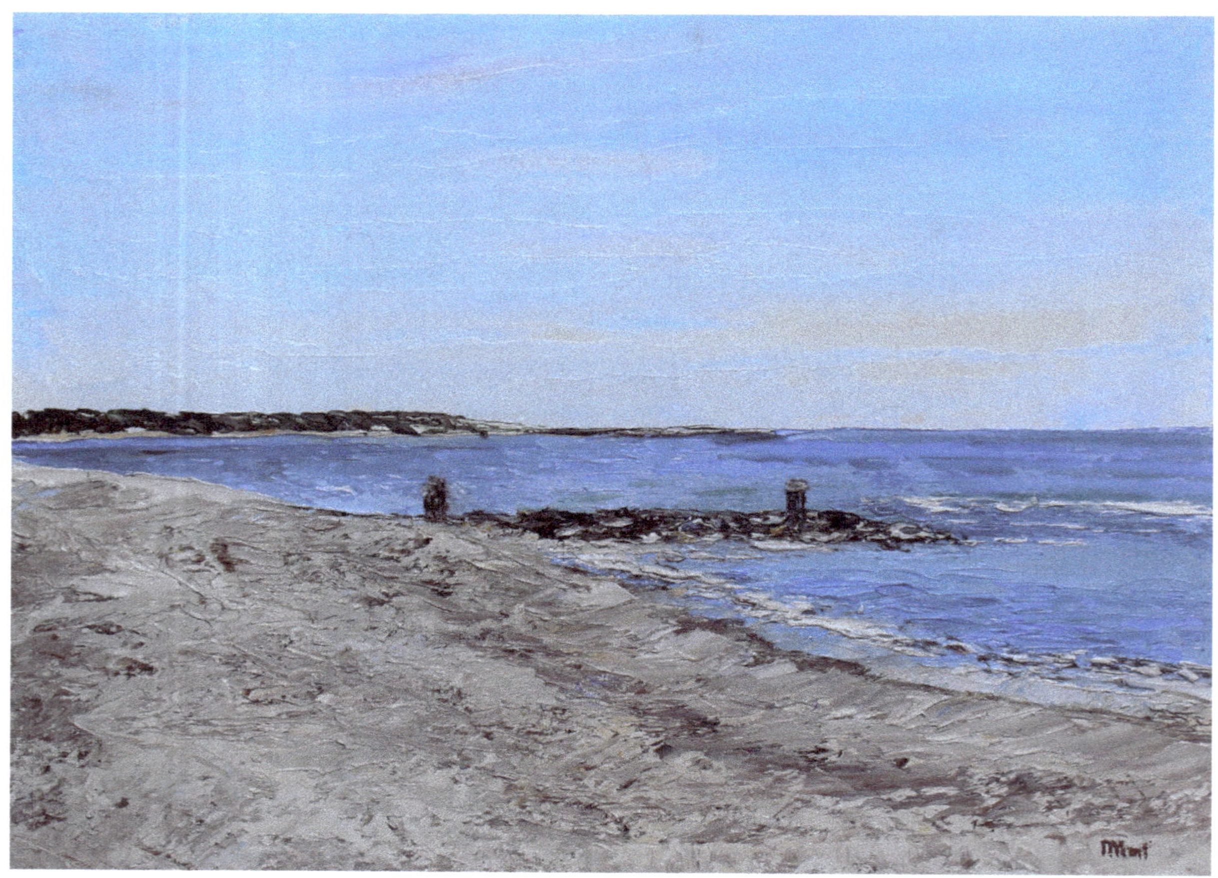

Menauhant beach. Holy ground to me. See pages 70 to learn why. Scan the QR code on page 66 to watch a video of this painting being created.

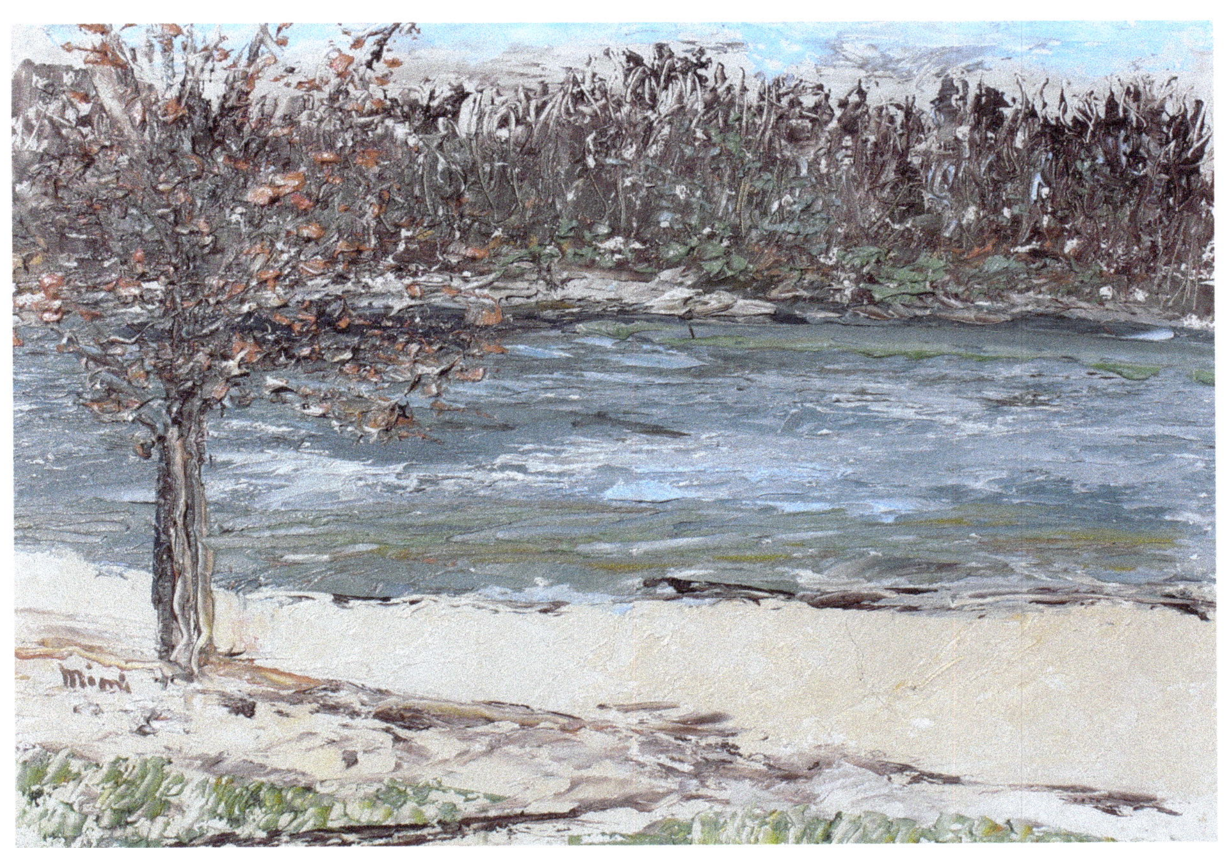

When I think "beach" I think saltwater and bay, but the Falmouth beach committee lists this beach as one of theirs so it's on my painting list! Which do you prefer? Salt water or freshwater ponds?

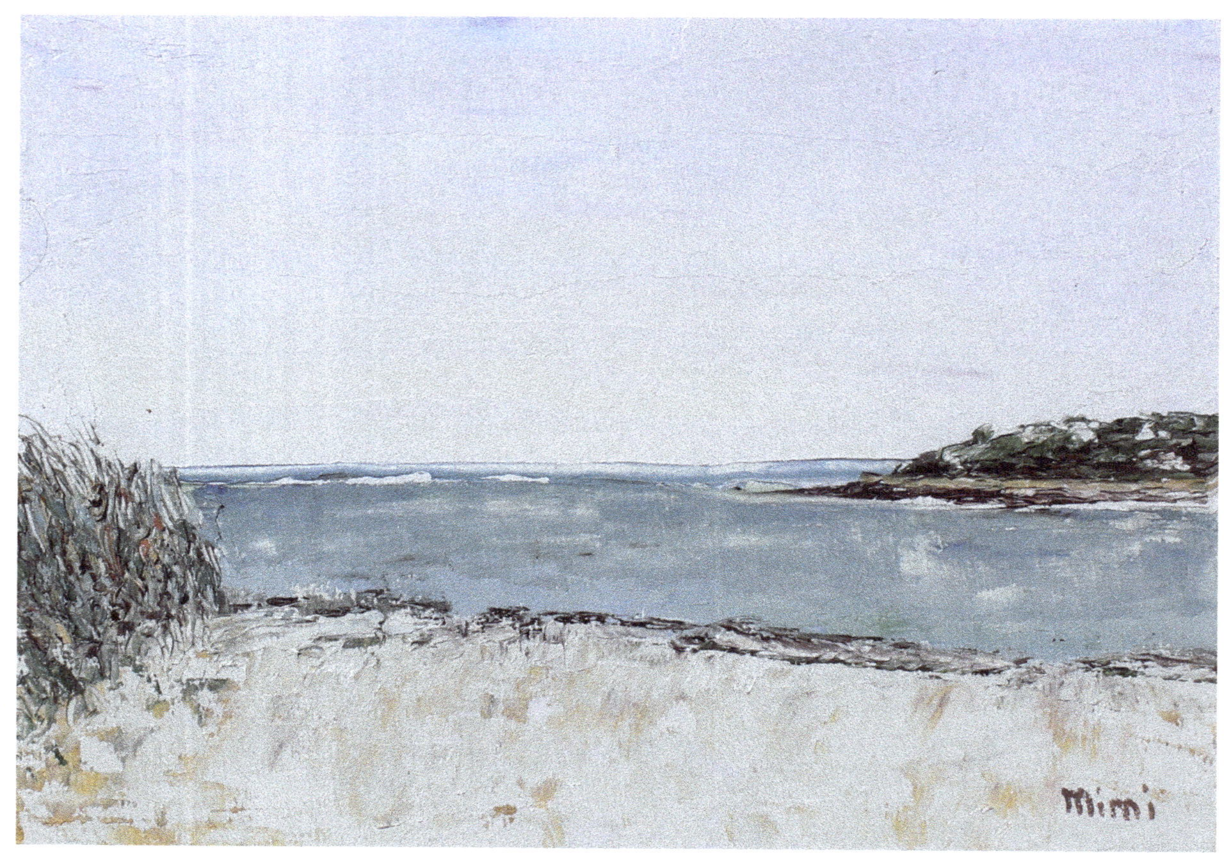

Overcast and a bit of fog today so a muted palette. Starting the second time around to each beach. Today it is Megansett. It's going to be fun to watch things turn green over the next several weeks!

DAY 12, APRIL 12 - CHAPOQUOIT BEACH

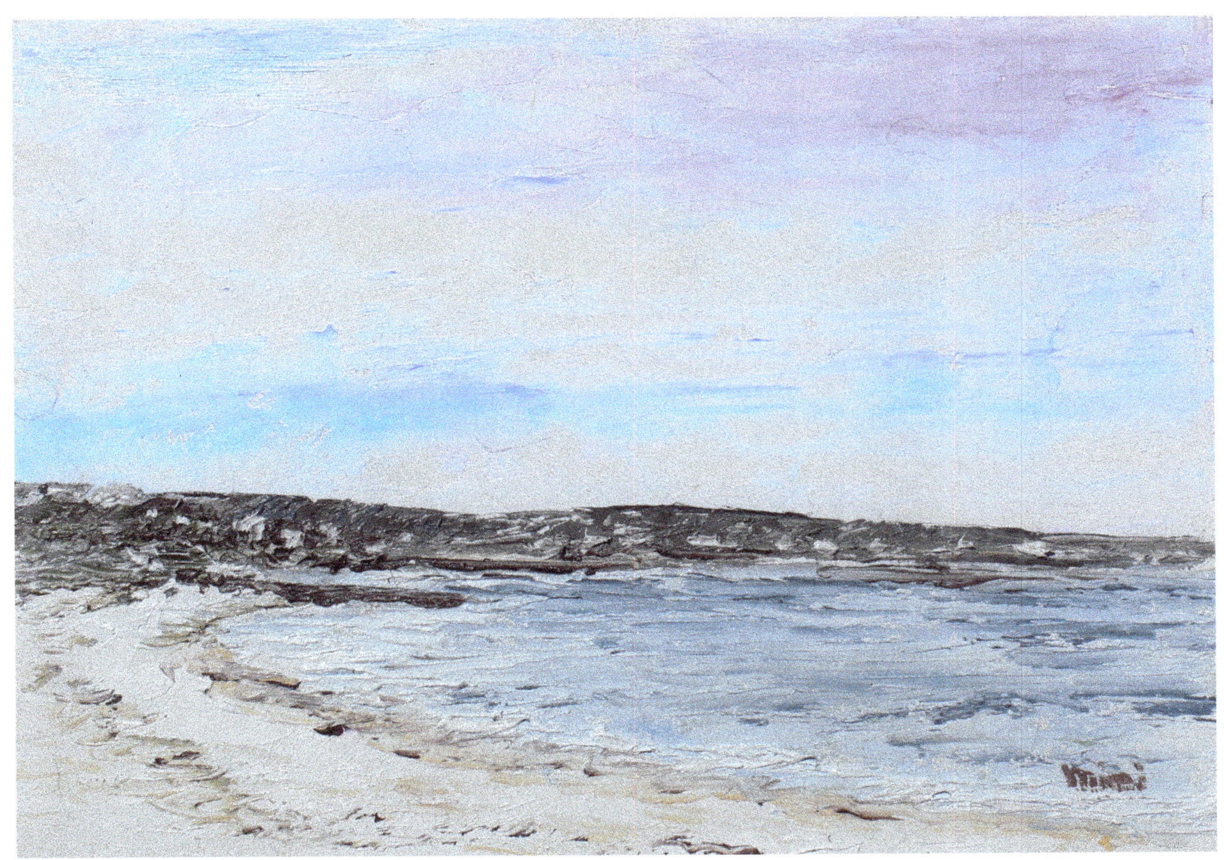

Wild skies over the water. Beauty in nature that an artist can only hope to capture its essence.

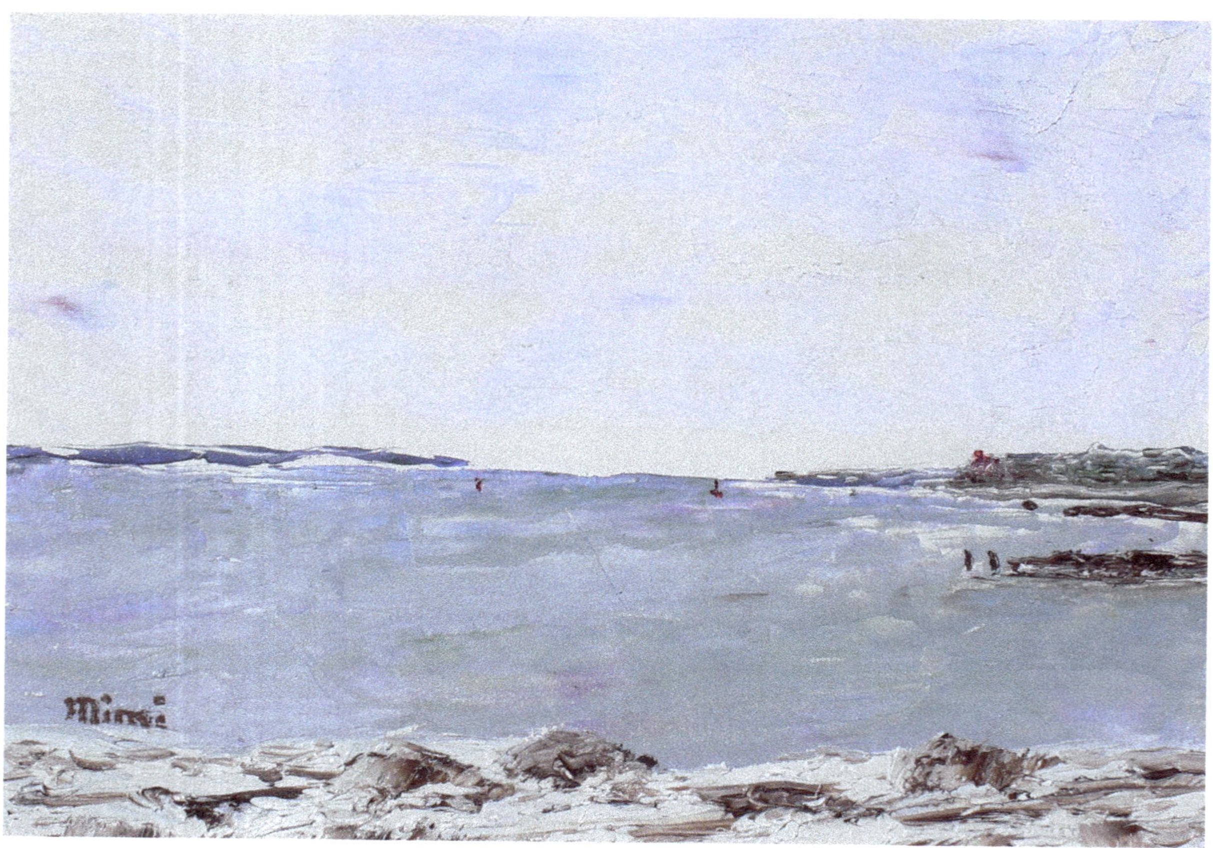

Back to Menauhant Beach. This time looking to the right, west southwest. Amazing how on a cloudy day the light refracts in a way that makes distant items crystal clear. Could see Nobska. And two red buoys in the middle of Nantucket Sound! Anyone who has navigated a boat in these waters knows those buoys, as one of them has no light or bell. So at night, someone has to be on the bow of the boat with a flashlight and lots of fingers crossed and prayers to find it before it finds the boat!

DAY 14, APRIL 14 - FALMOUTH HEIGHTS BEACH

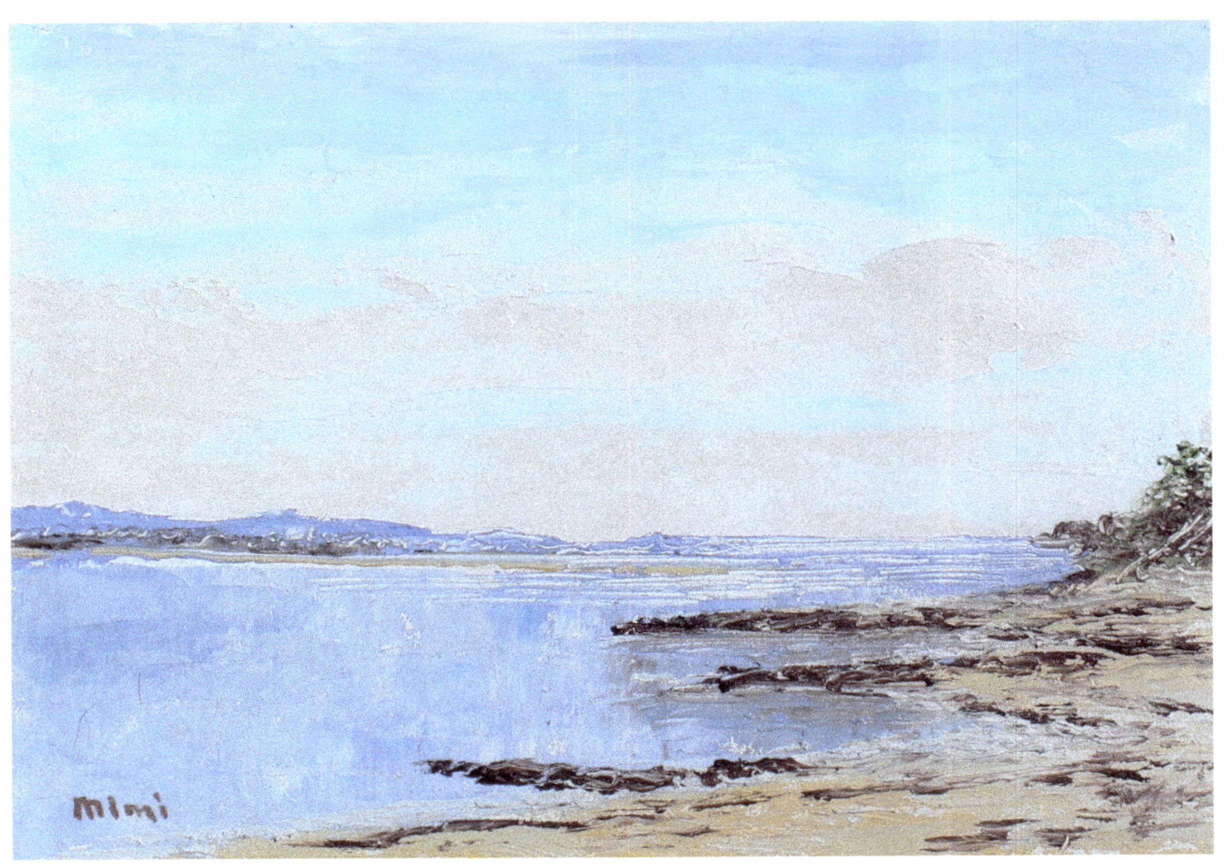

Beautiful sunlight today.

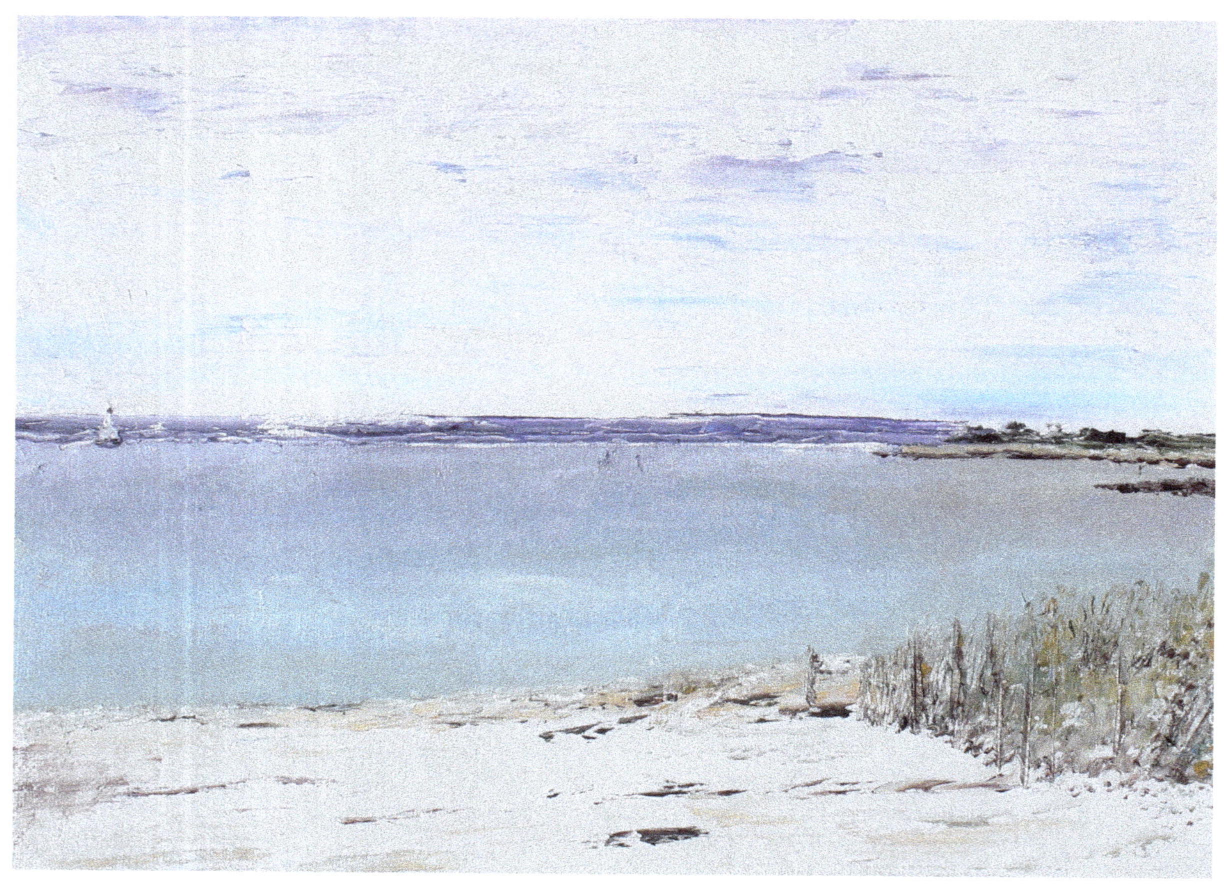

Second time around the beaches. A grey Thursday afternoon.

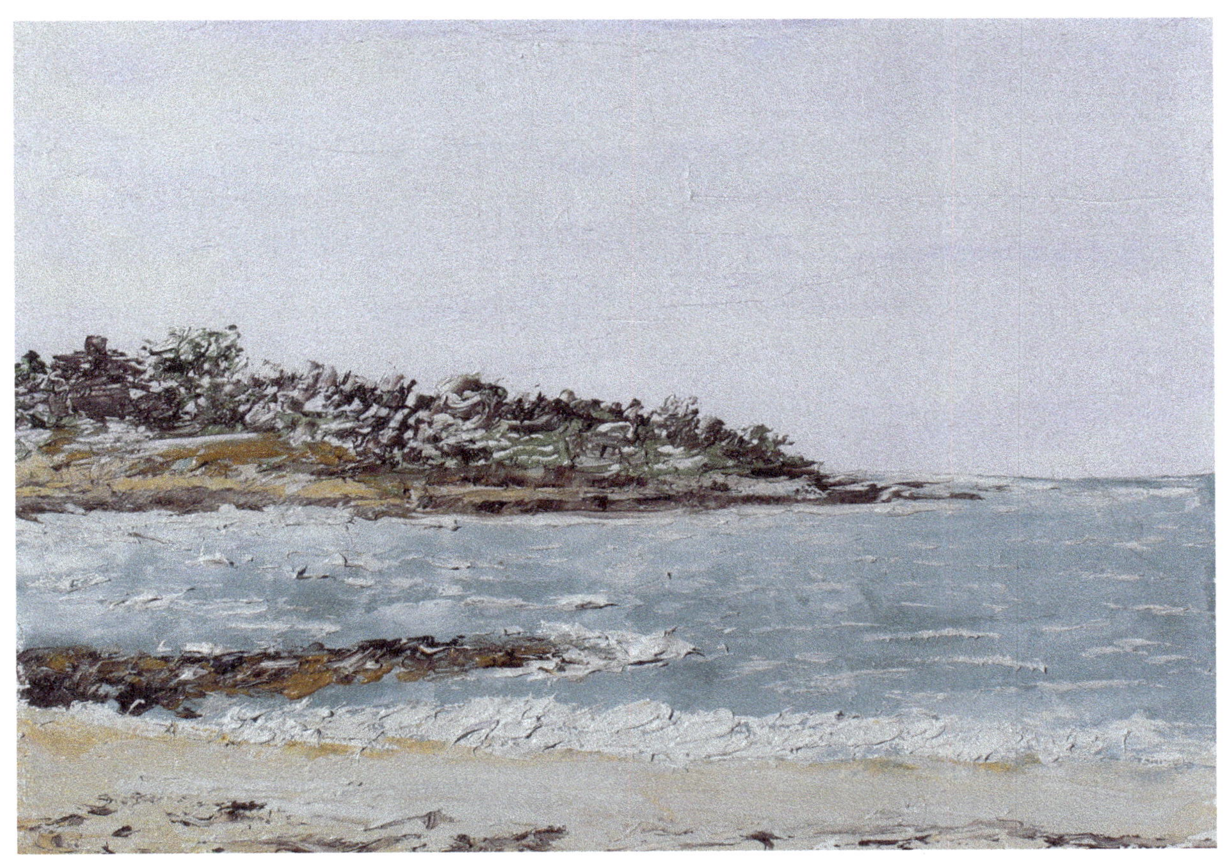

Scan the QR code on page 67 to watch a video and hear about the conditions of the day this painting was created.

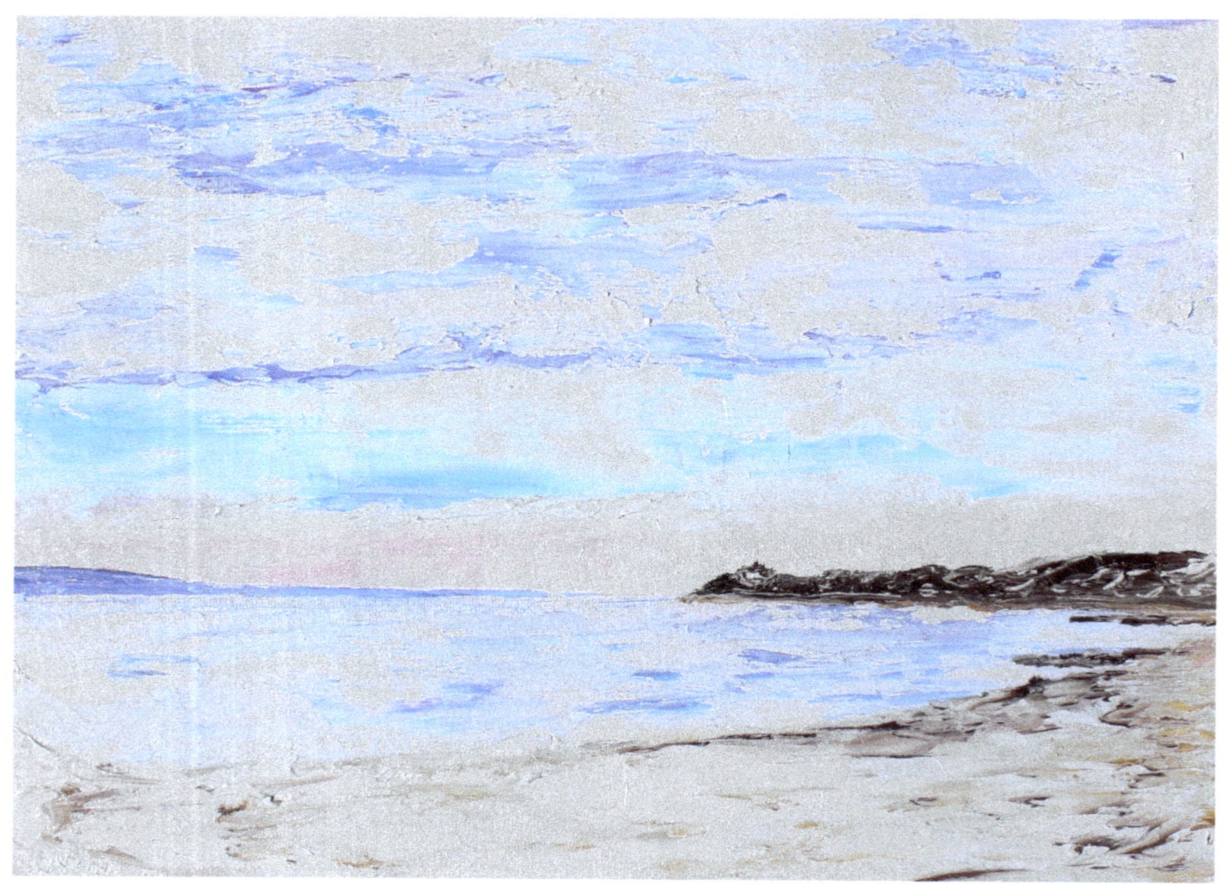

Oh the skies were so fun to watch. Dark clouds. Light clouds. And everything in between. This painted around 5pm.

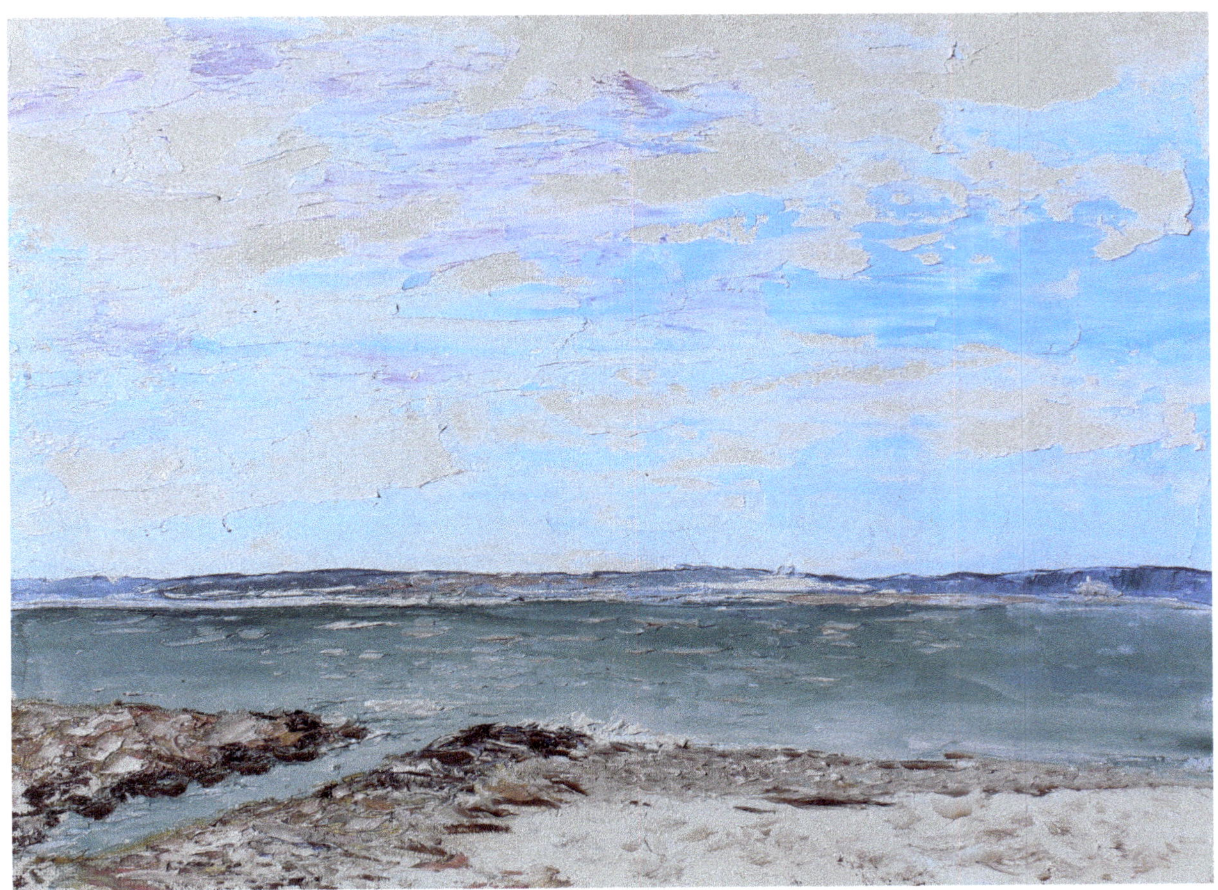

Today is one third of the way through the project! The sky was stormy, over bright blue, with dark green water. Beautiful. What will YOU create today? Bring joy. Share love. Another time lapse video for you on page 67 of today's painting in the creative process.

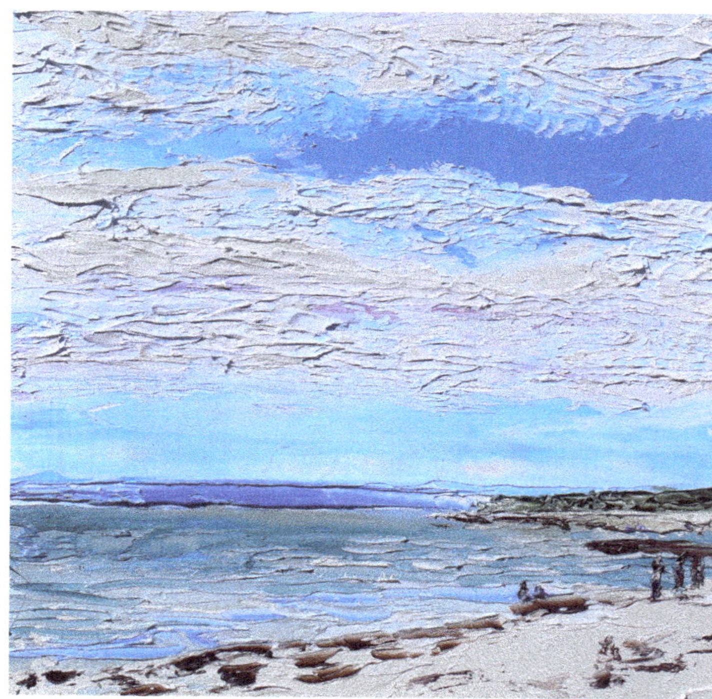

Woodneck Beach. Finger painting. It's not just for kids. Puffy clouds. After using the painting knife I played with some finger painting to soften edges. And was able to shoot a video real time of the fun. Scan the QR code on page 67 to watch a little bit of it. No soundtrack. Just the quiet. Breathe.

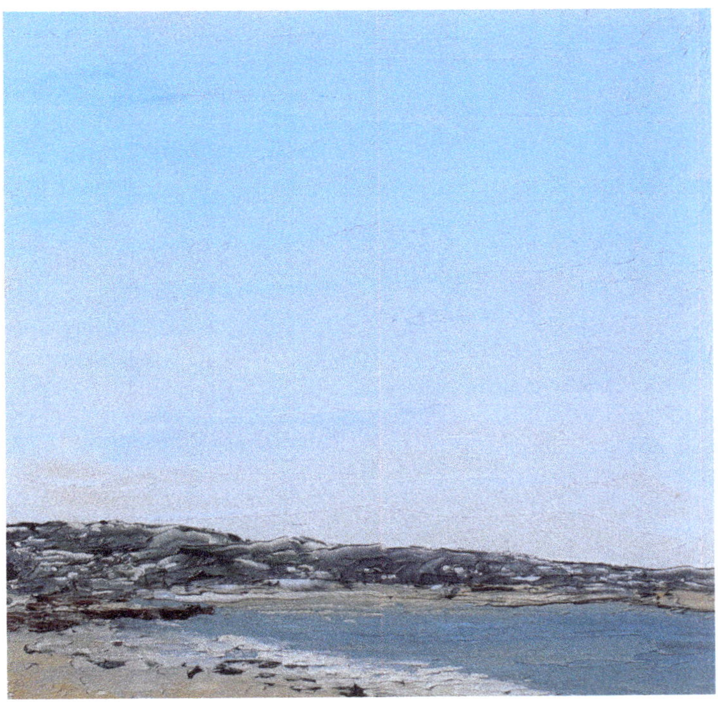

Sunshine and blue skies. Back to Chapoquoit Beach for the 3rd round. Went minimalist today. Not a cloud in the sky.

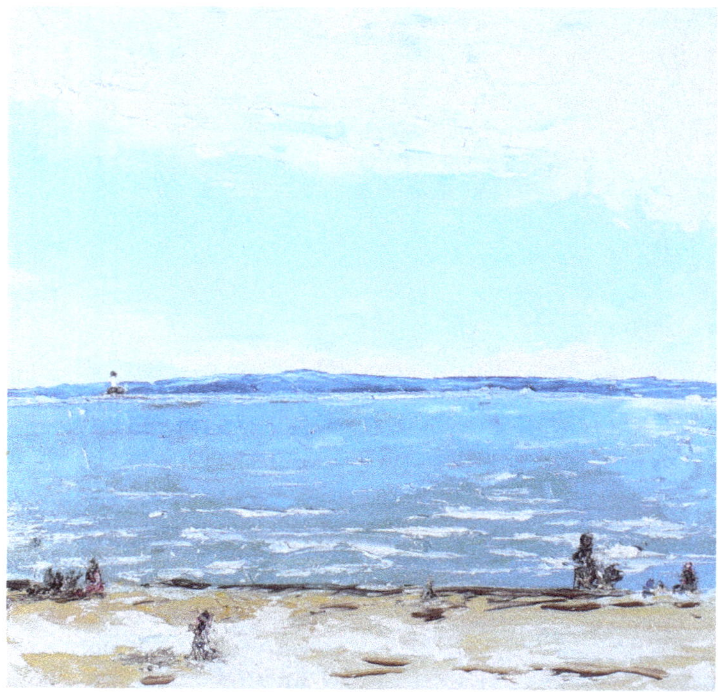

School break week. Little clusters of little ones playing on the beach. A preview of the months to come. The wind off the water was a bit cold, so still lots of dark warm clothing. Not time for bathing suites quite yet. Painted at Old Silver, this beach scene really could be anywhere, couldn't it? Except for the distinctive shape of Cleveland Ledge lighthouse in the distance.

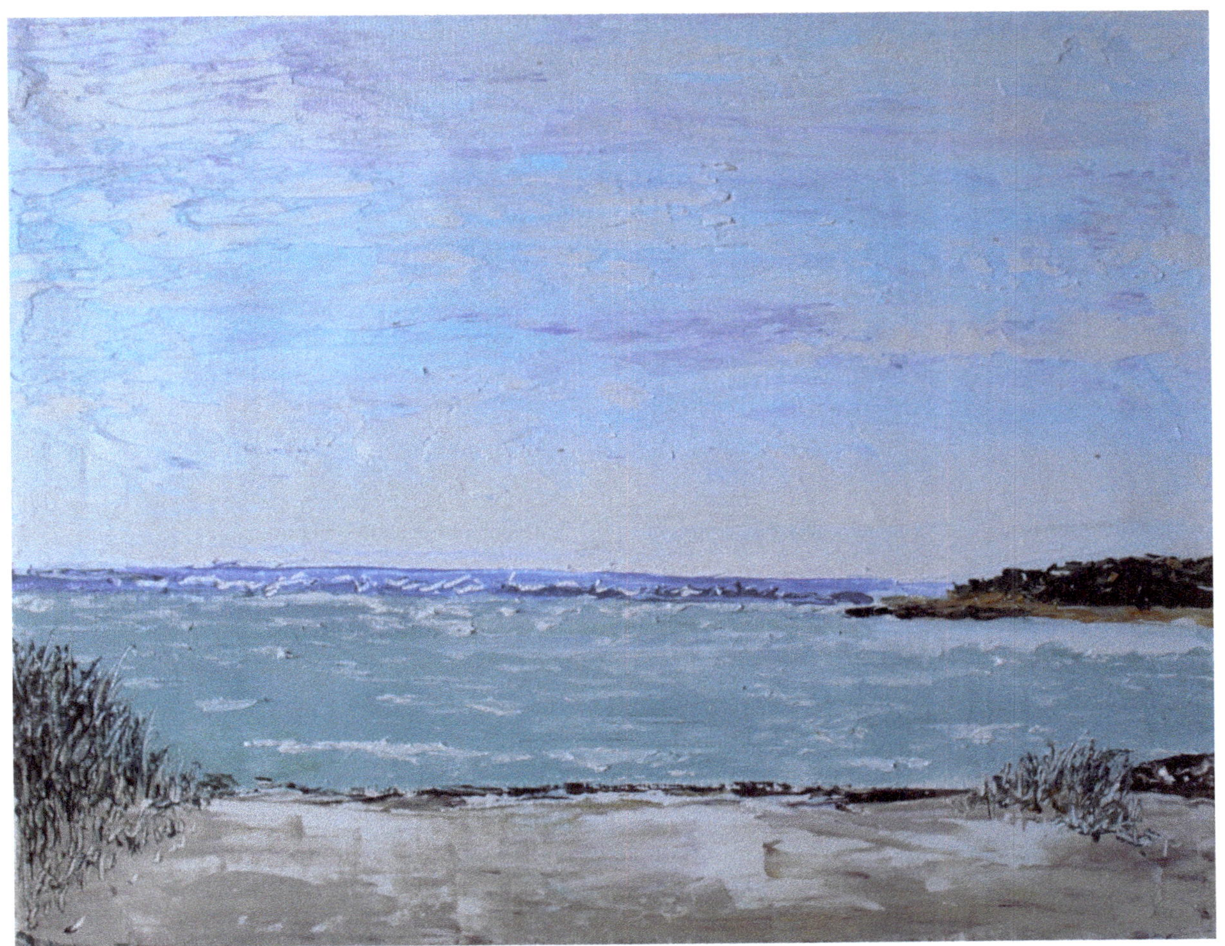

The wind was howling, the waves were rolling in, and I painted two instead of one.

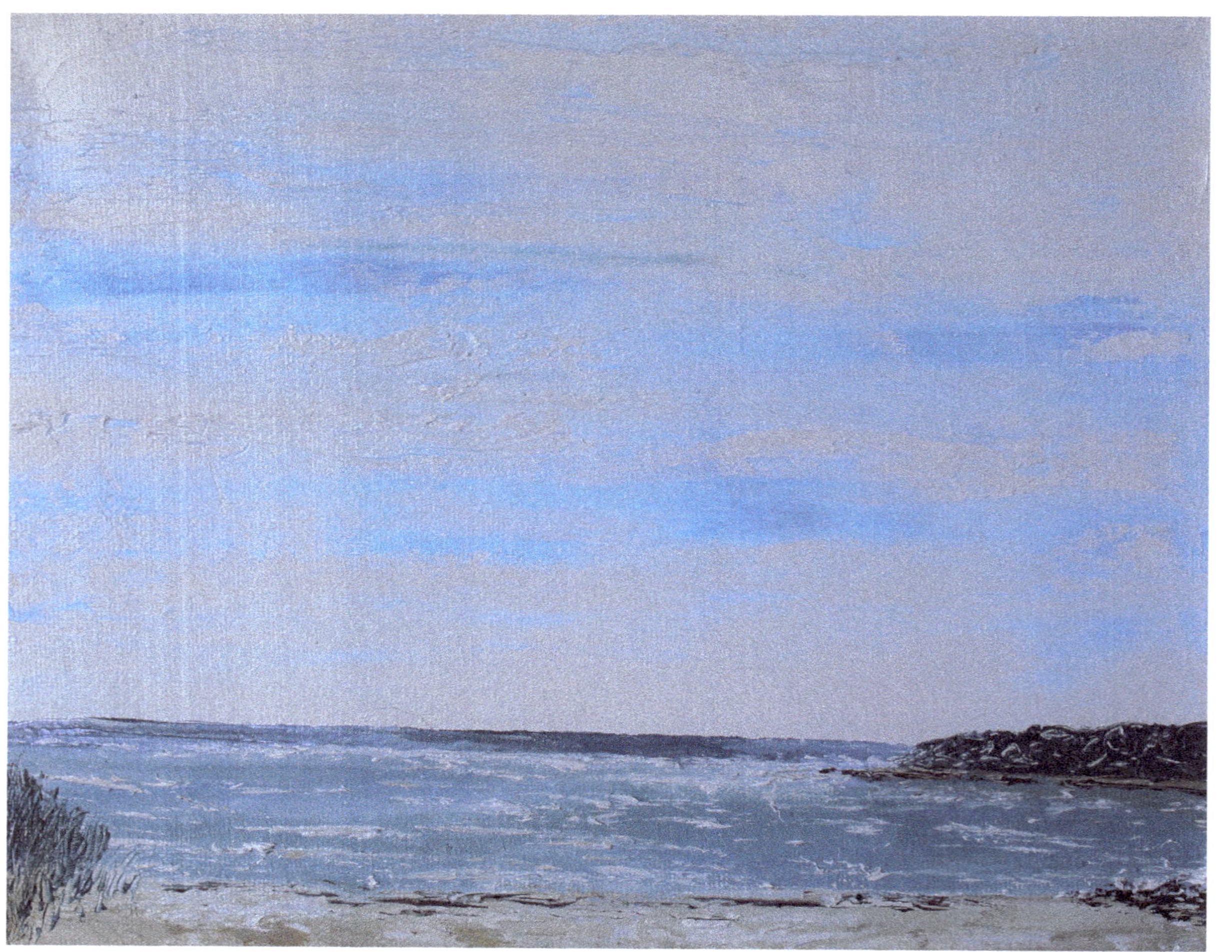

Second painting, same day. Funny observation. A family got out of their car, with their dog, and ran out onto the beach, in spite of how hard the sand was blowing. The dog turned and ran back to the car, as if to say "You folks have got to be kidding - that sand HURTS! Let me back in the car!"

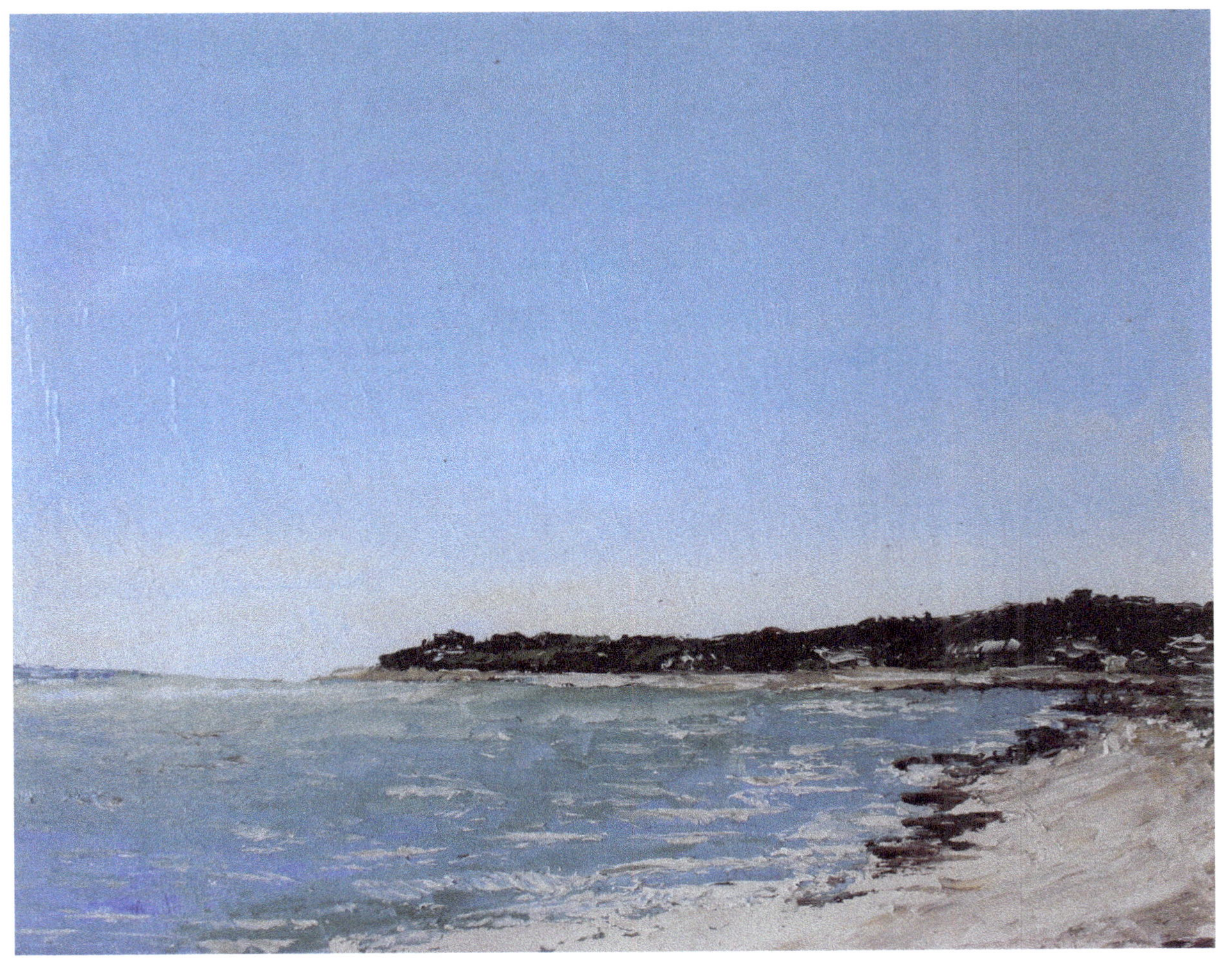

Wild winds and blowing sand, again. Had the sunroof open just a little and somehow the sand found its way up and in. Look closely. There are grains of sand in the paint! I suppose that makes it an authentic Cape Cod beach painting?

One of the joys of having a 'mobile studio' set up in the front seat of my car is the opportunity to paint impromptu. Though I did my 'official' painting of the day this morning, I ended up back at the beach early evening, and was blown away (pun intended) by the beauty and intensity of the waves and surf as far as the eye could see, and the green color of the water that we only see this time of year. Grabbed a 5"x7" canvas board, and did a very quick impressionist knife painting bordering on abstract. Didn't even worry about covering the entire canvas with paint.

Fun and exhilarating as the process of creating art should be.

While yes, I sell my paintings as a way to pay life's expenses, another theme for me for many years has been to encourage others to explore their own creative endeavors, FOR THE JOY OF IT. Creativity is healing, restorative, relaxing, and yes, sacred. When we create, tension leaves the body, our breathing slows, we connect with something... other.

Much more to say on this topic another time. For now, I will simply share the painting I did this evening. There is a QR code on page 67 to take you to the video of the surf that inspired it.

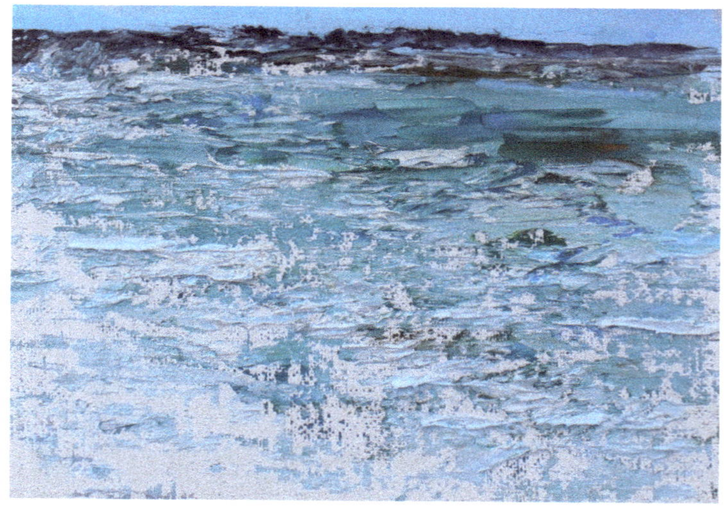

DAY 24, APRIL 24 - STONEY BEACH IN WOODS HOLE

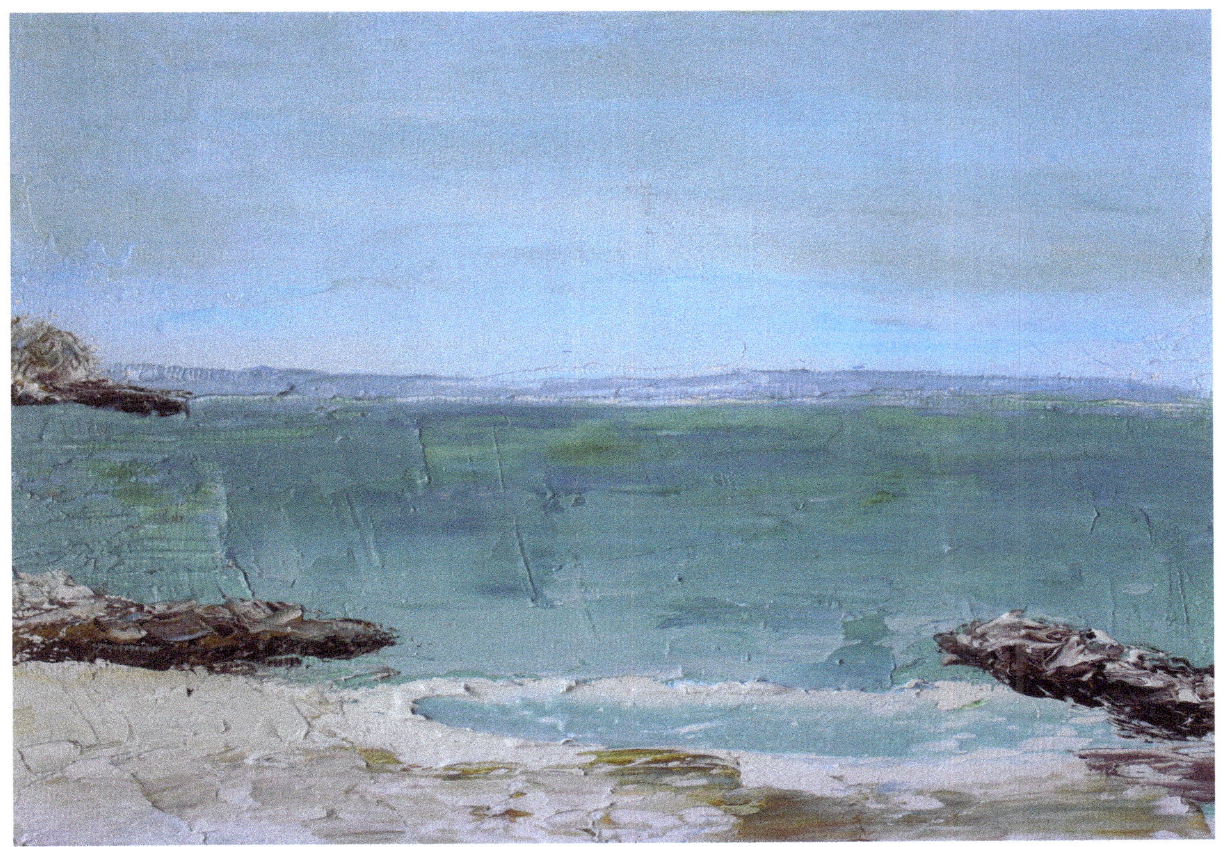

The other two times I painted here it was wild winds and rain. Thought it would be good to revisit on a sunny day like today.

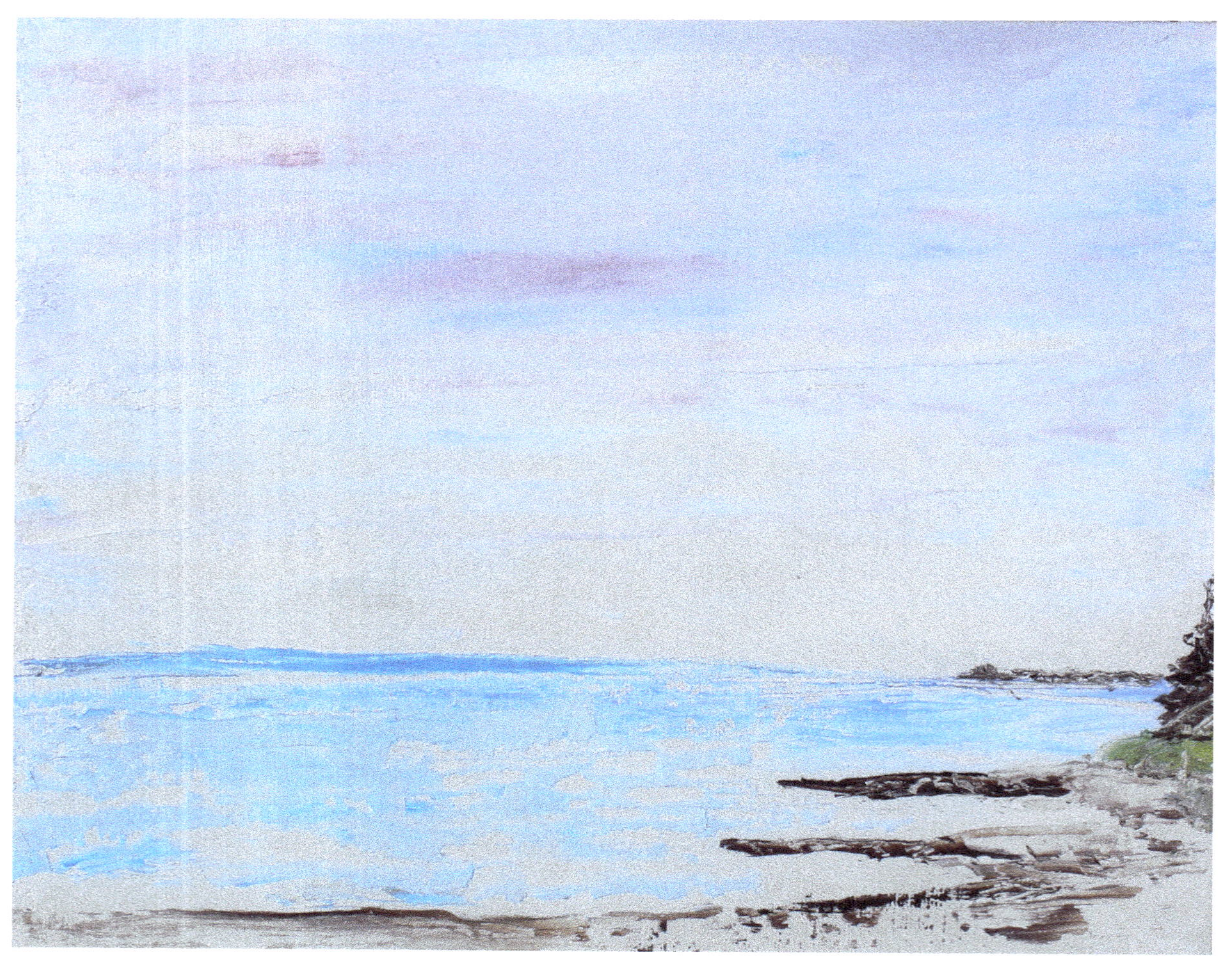

A cold, dreary, foggy April day. Had to draw on memory of what it looked like on a brighter day. Kinda like our moods sometimes. When thoughts go dreary, refocus on gratitude for blessings of joy that have been, are, and will be again.

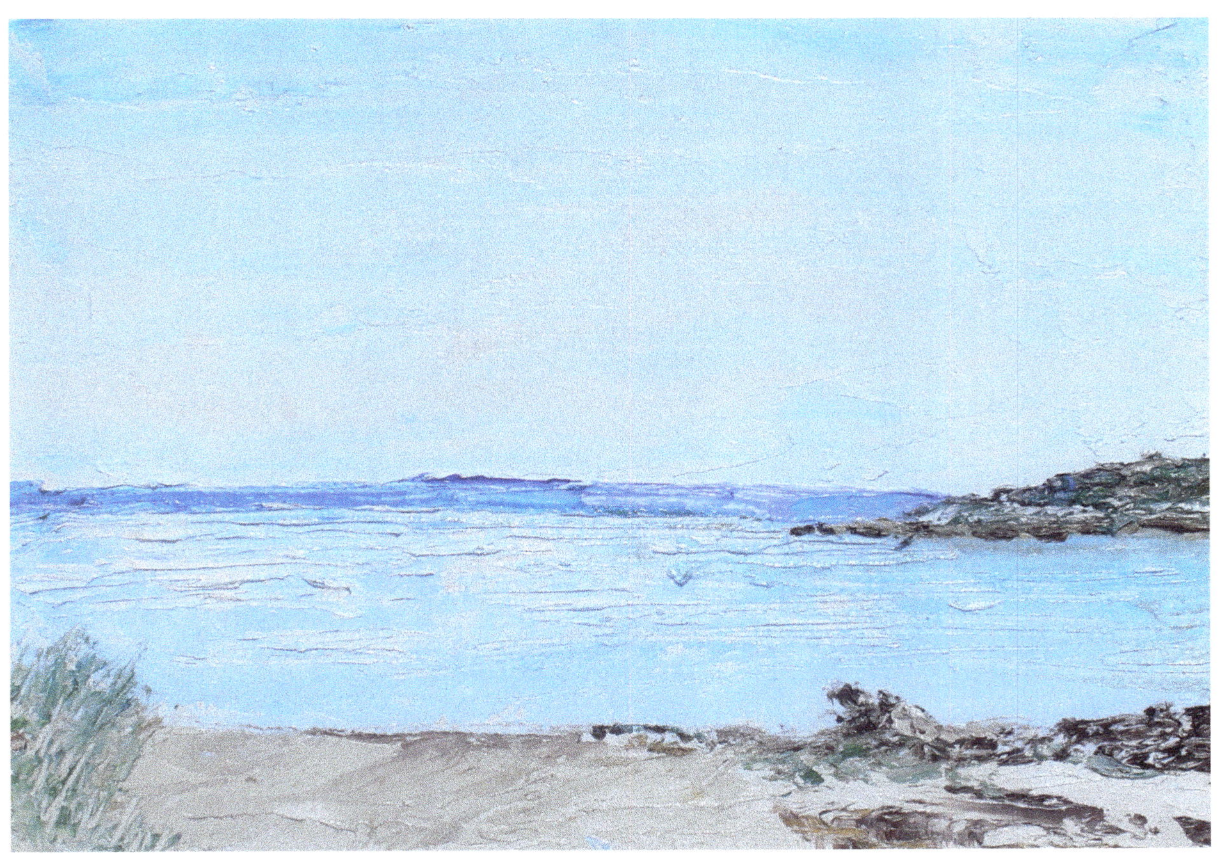

Back at Megansett because, well, sometimes I just have to. It's magical to me.

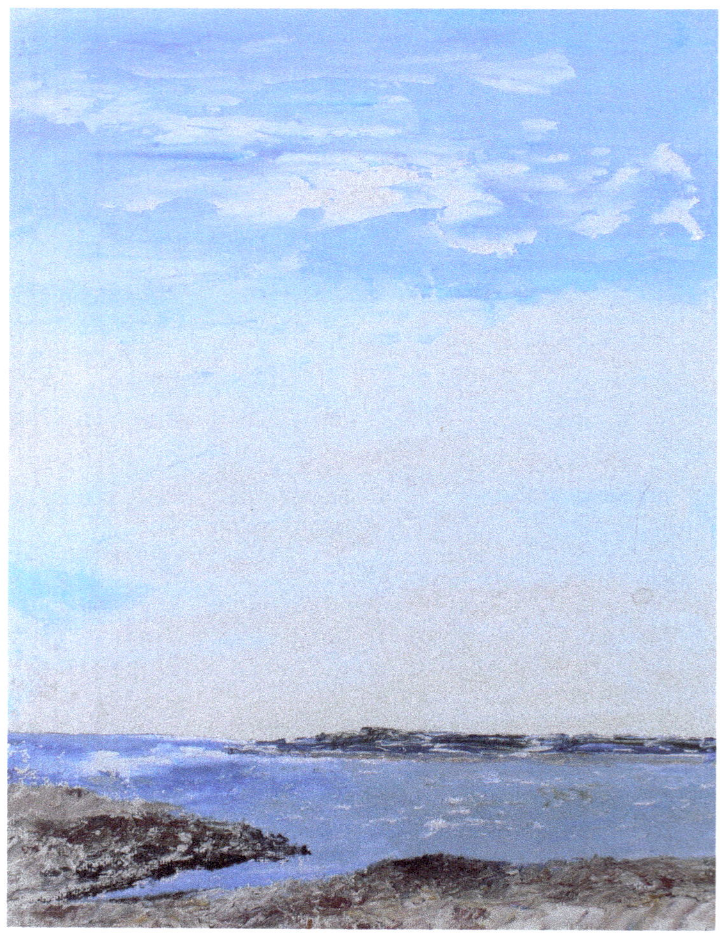

HALFWAY! Went for a vertical orientation rather than horizontal. Oh, what a BEAUTIFUL day!

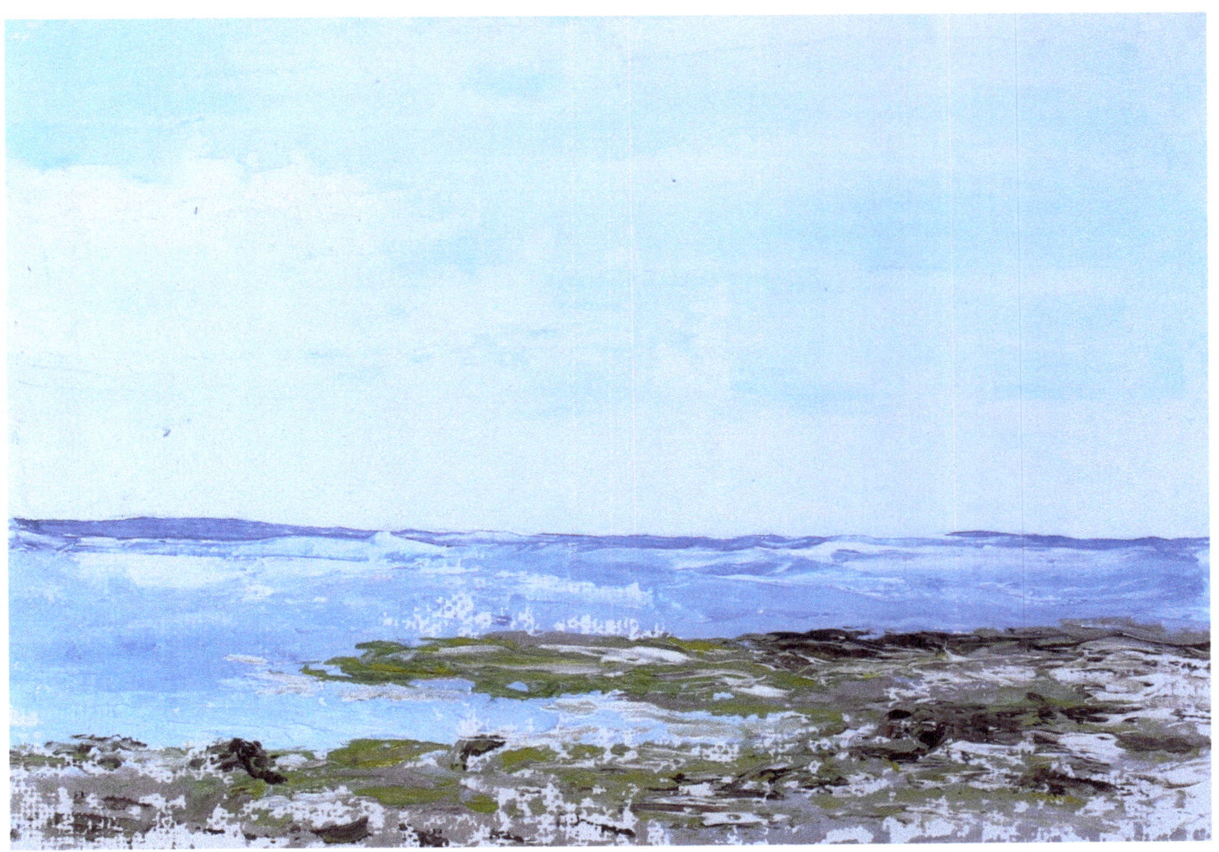

Also did a second smaller quick one because the sandbar was so pretty with some green showing. Enjoy! Scan the QR code on page 67 to hear comments from me about this day.

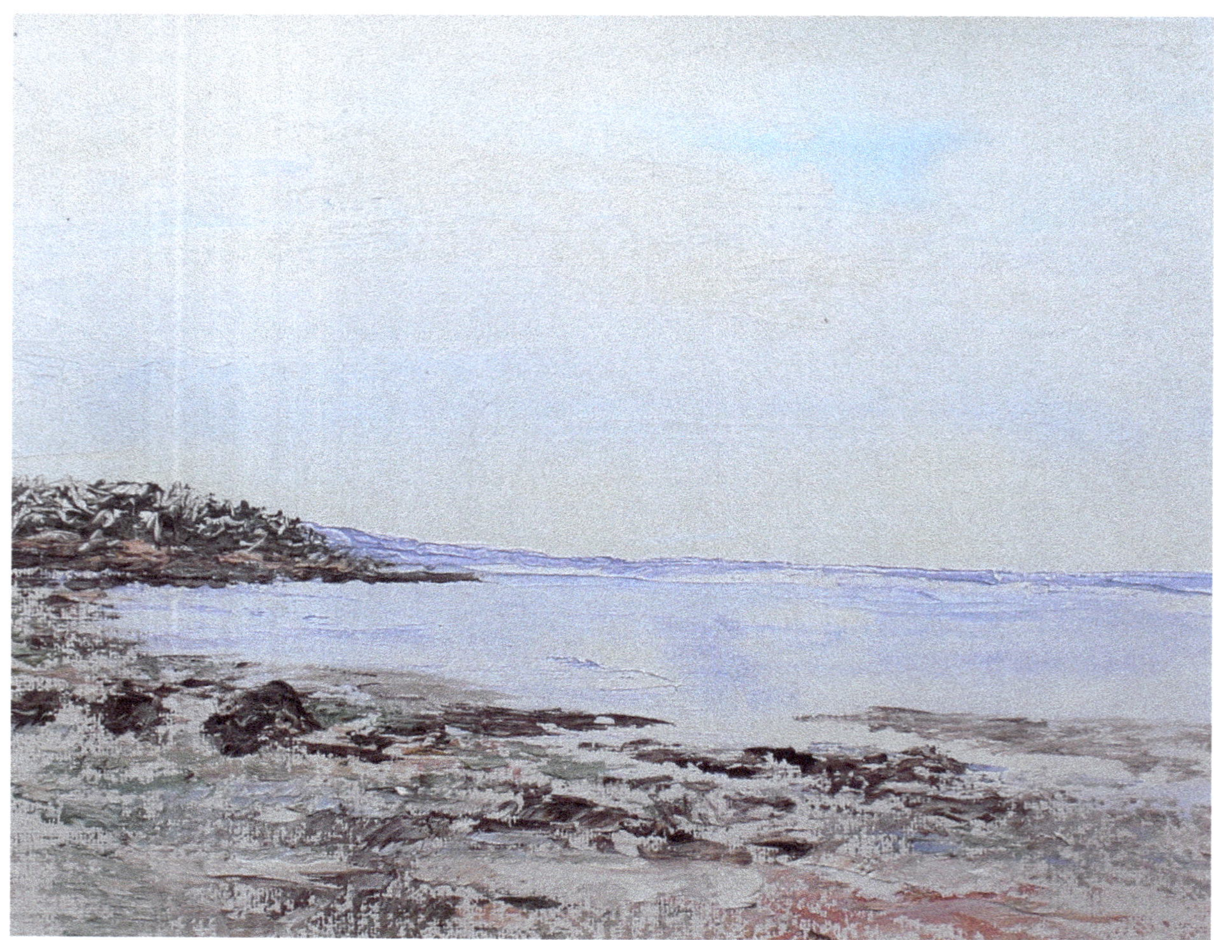

So beautiful today at Woodneck Beach. Most days I'm painting from the front seat of my car but today it is warmer, and less windy, so I can venture out onto the sand. Well, that, and the fact that you can't really SEE the beach from the parking lot at Woodneck. I'm also learning that it is ok to not cover the entire canvas with paint.

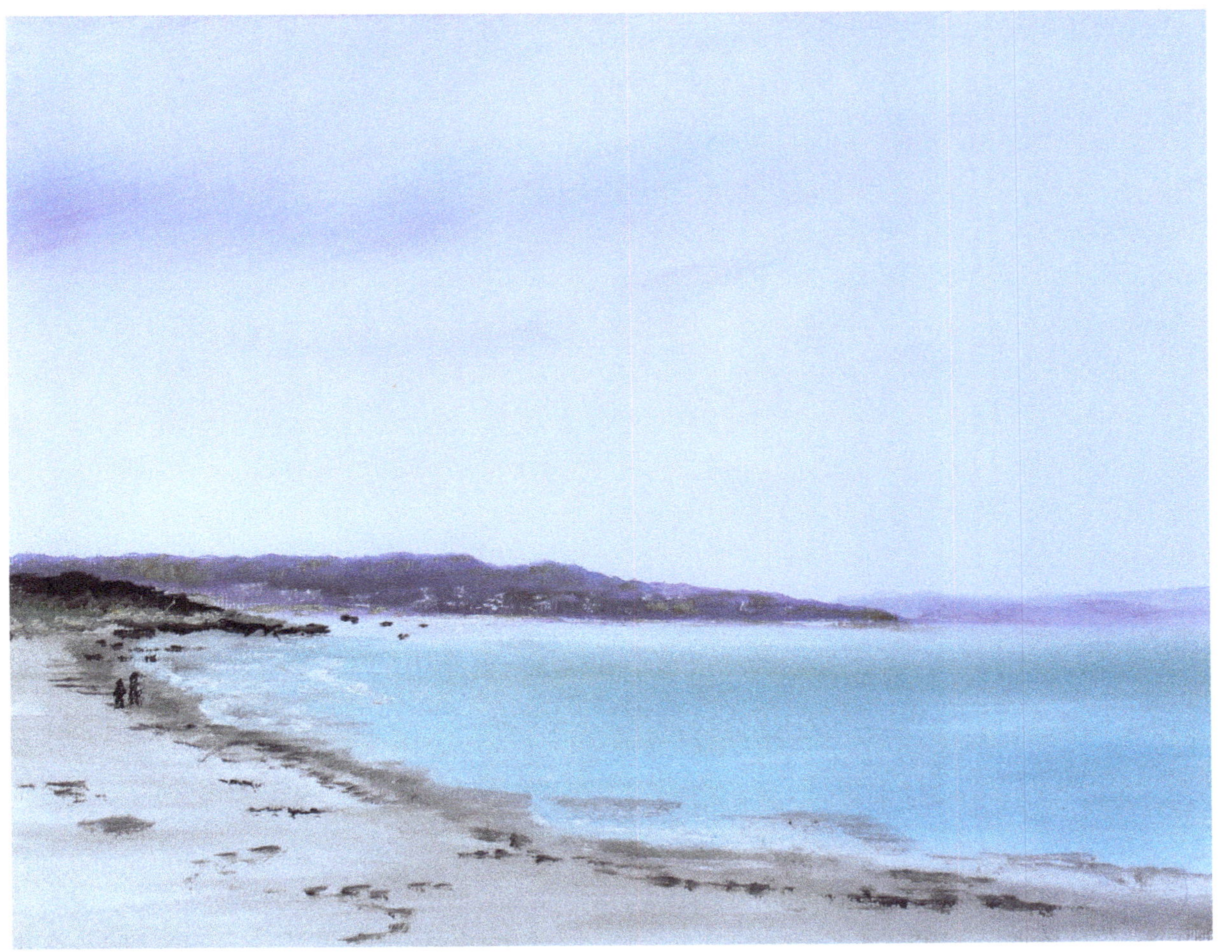

Chapoquoit Beach on a misty, overcast (ok, yes, rainy) day. Subdued colors. I felt the nudge to paint old school today, with brushes, rather than palette knife. Kinda like it. Different than the others. Later note: This painting was hands down the favorite on social media, which I find kinda funny, because it was quite literally painted through the windshield wipers.

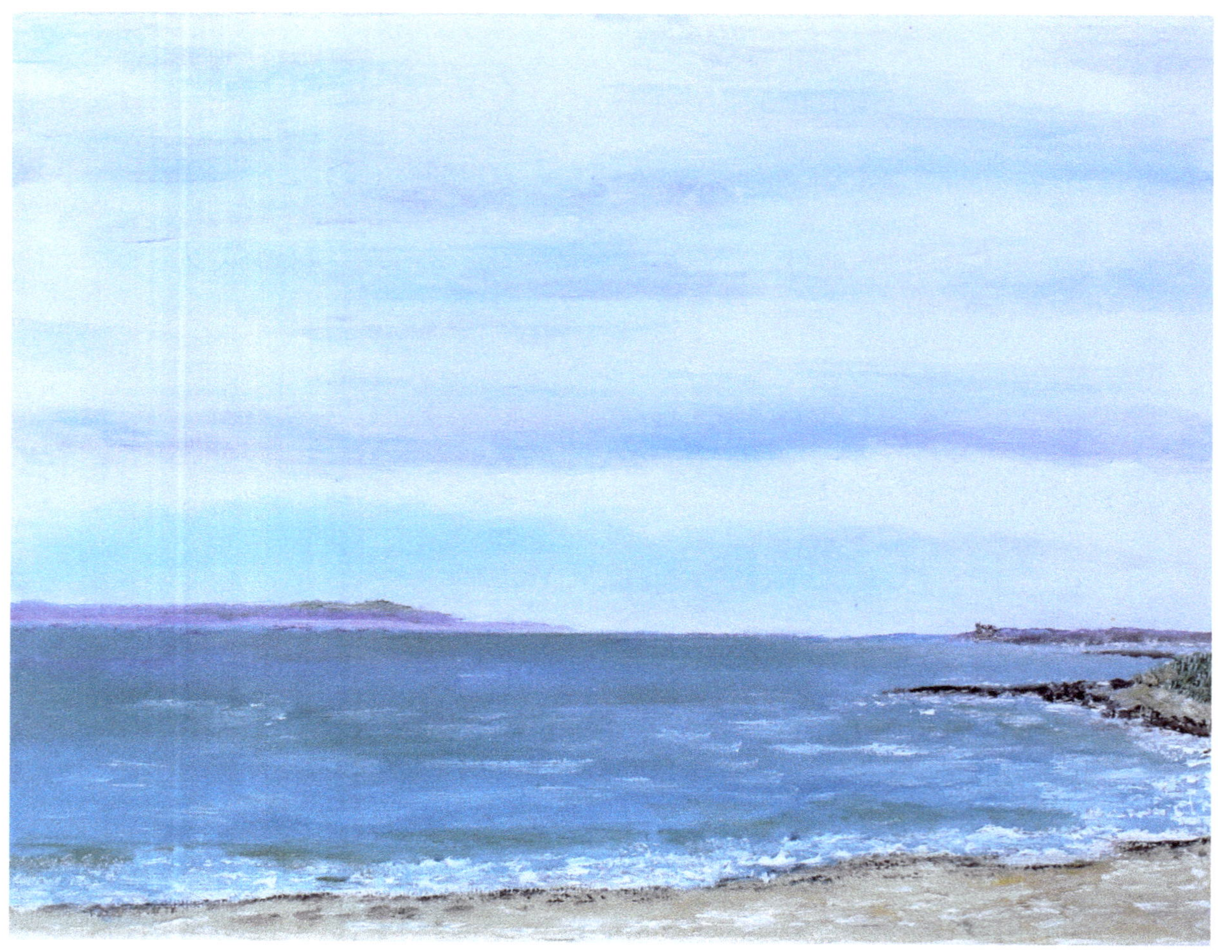

Two paintings today. One with brushes, the other with palette knife. Do you prefer one over the other? This is the first one, painted with traditional paint brushes.

DAY 30, APRIL 30 - MENAUHANT BEACH

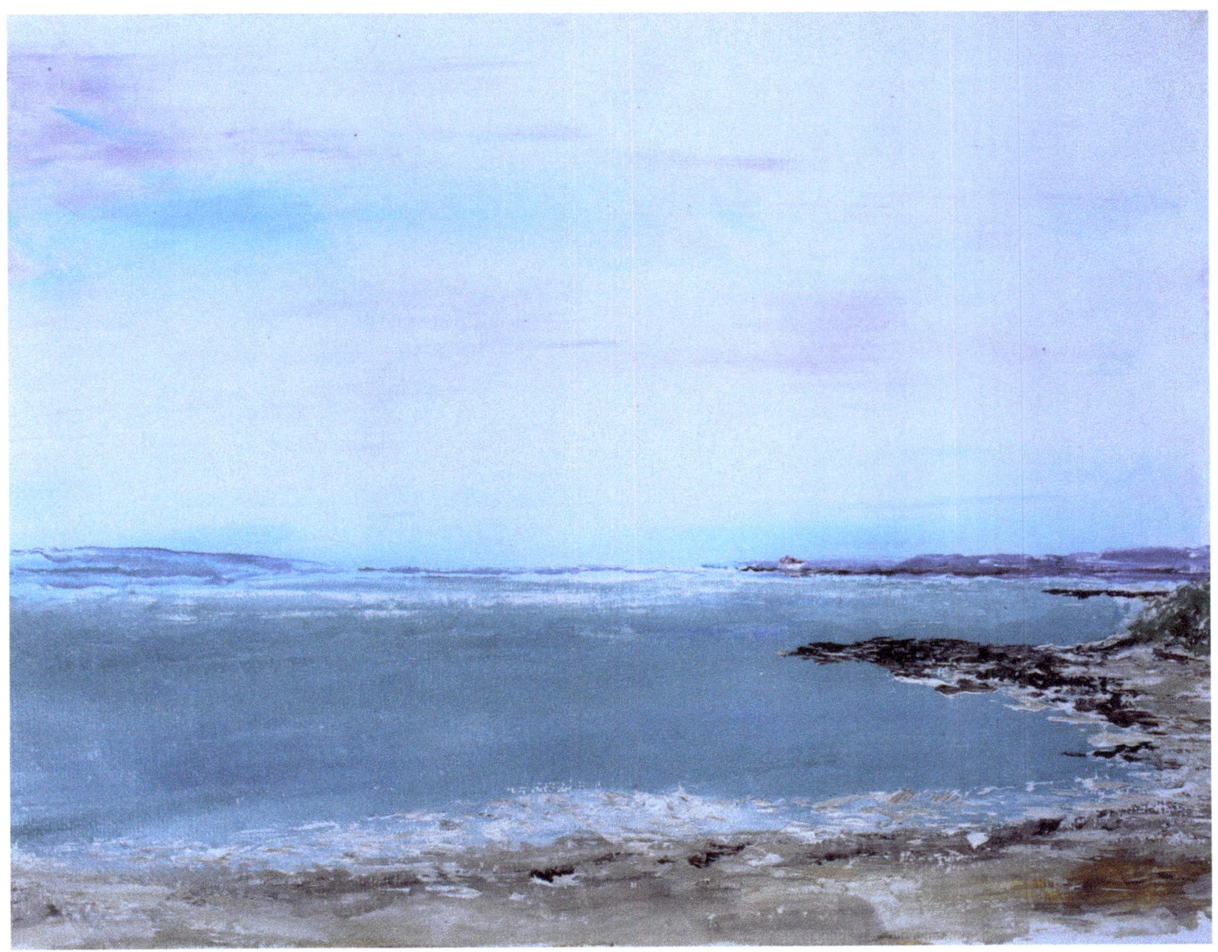

This is the second one, painted with palette knife. So grateful to all for so many lovely words of support and encouragement received both on social media posts, and in person. All helping to make fabulous Falmouth the place to be!

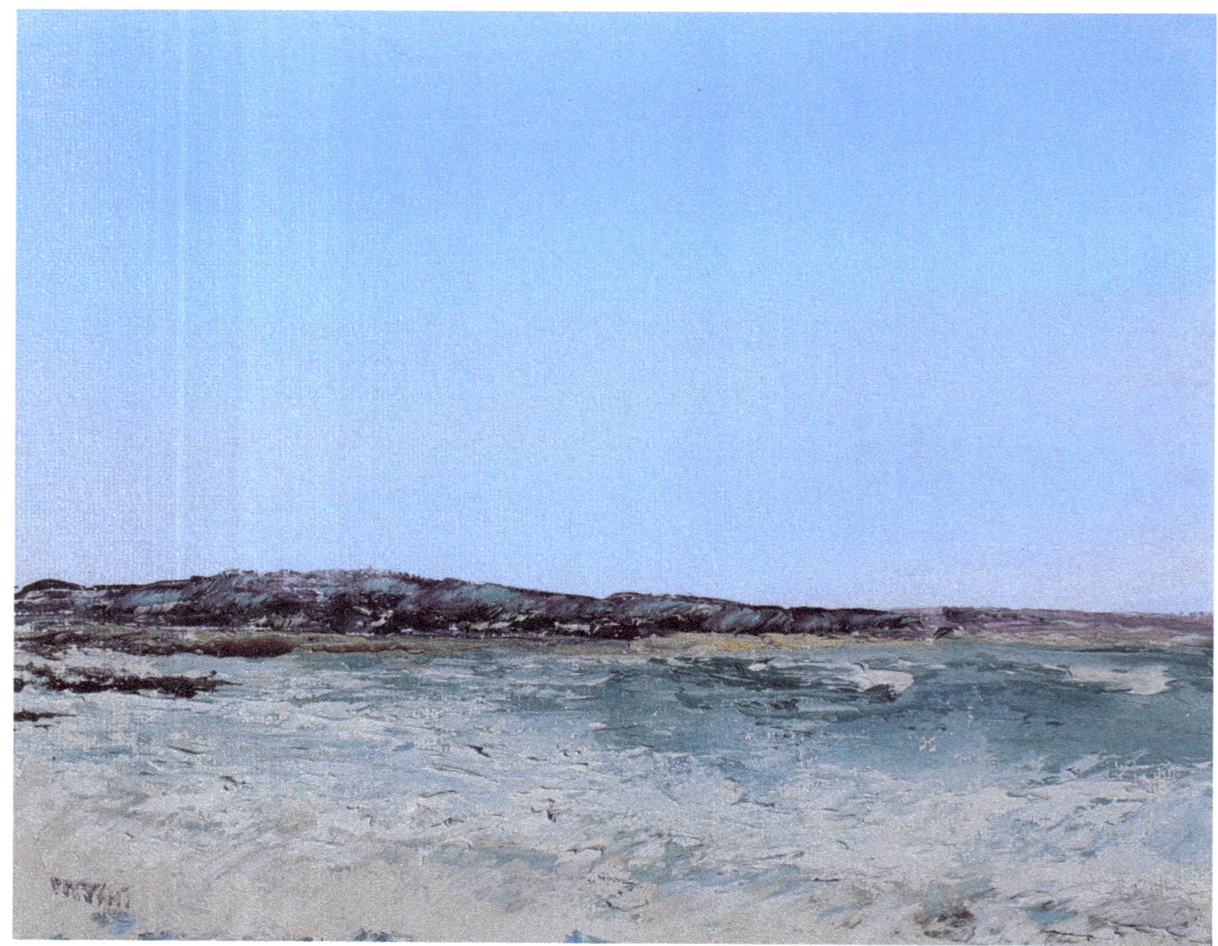

Wind blowing strong. A hybrid of brush painting (the sky) and palette knife (everything other than sky.) Later note: Funny thing. I remember it was painted with high emotion. And now, in hindsight, I don't even remember what it was that had me upset. Oh, if we could only remember, in the moment, how emotions pass, perhaps we would not allow them to upset us so much!

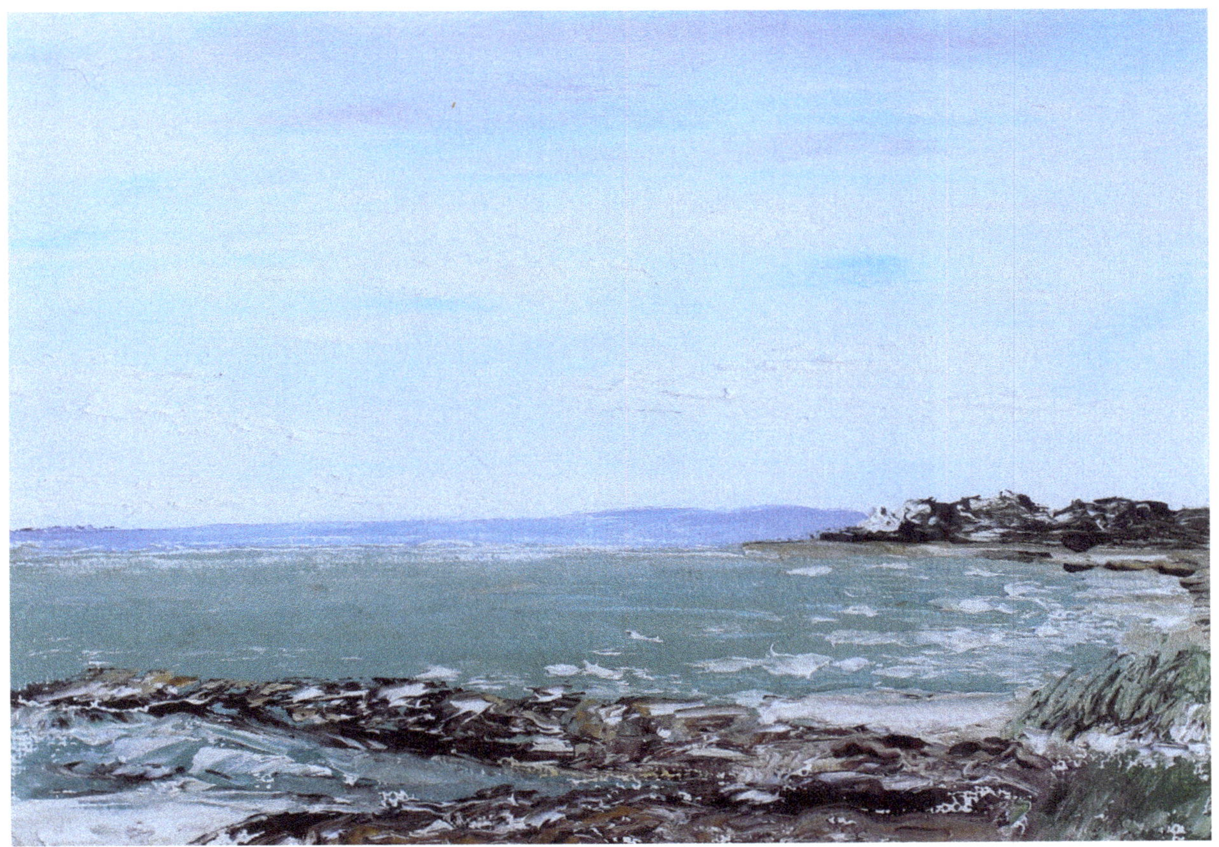

Old Silver Beach has two parking lots. This painted from the larger one, looking north across the jetties. A mix of brush and knife painting.

DAY 33, MAY 3 - CHAPOQUOIT BEACH

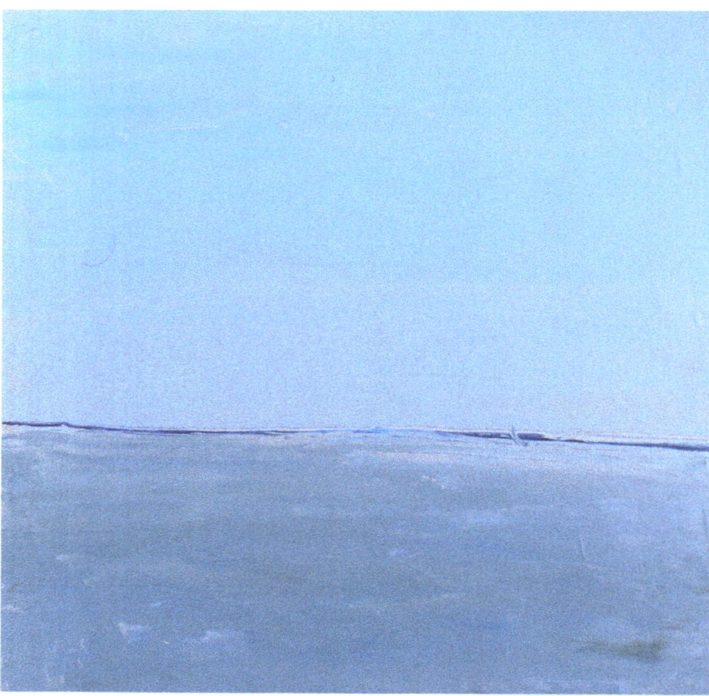

Today at Chapoquoit, though really could be anywhere. Looking straight ahead rather than to the right or the left (sounds like a political commentary but I assure you it is not.) No clouds. No waves. Only a single sailboat on the horizon. Minimalist. Calming.

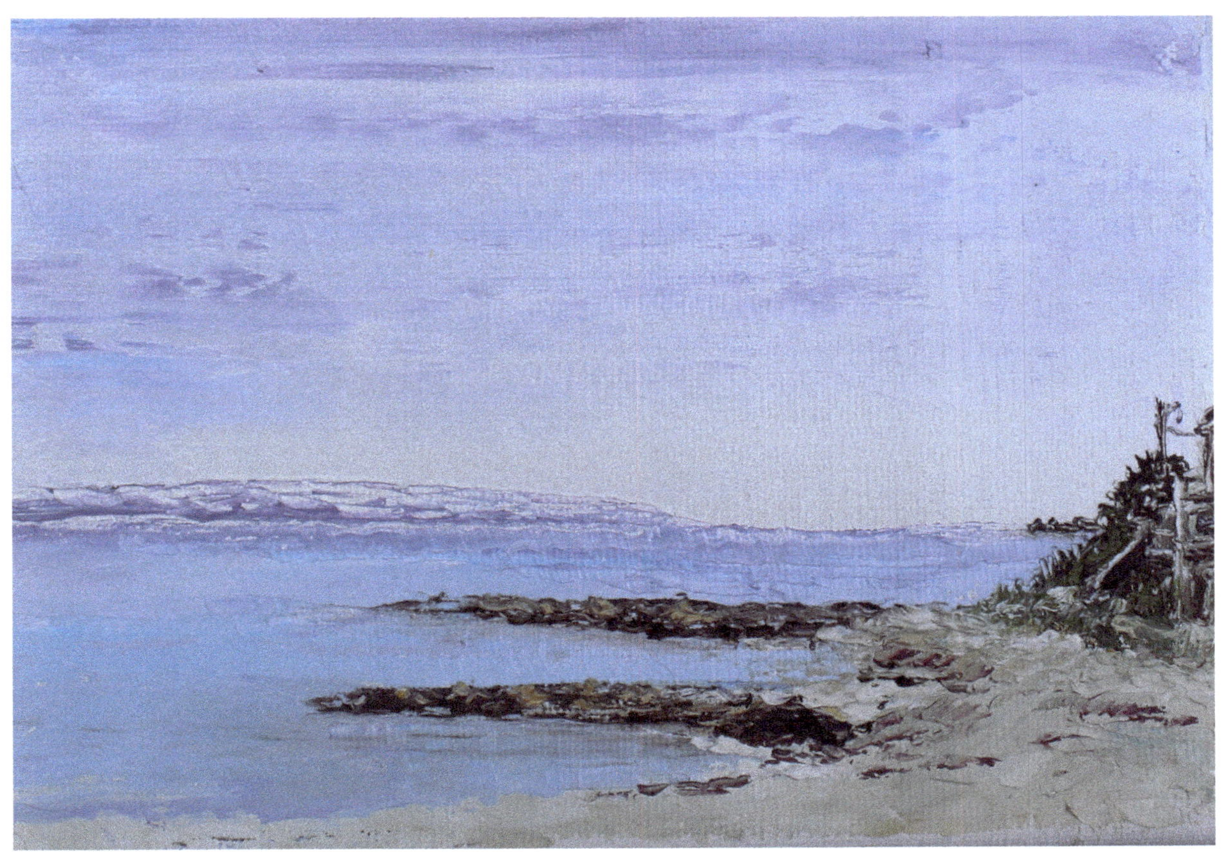

Challenging to paint 'pretty' on a gloomy weather day, but had fun painting more of the details up the beach to the far right. The stairs up the hill, and a hint of the Casino building.

DAY 35, MAY 5 - SURF DRIVE BEACH

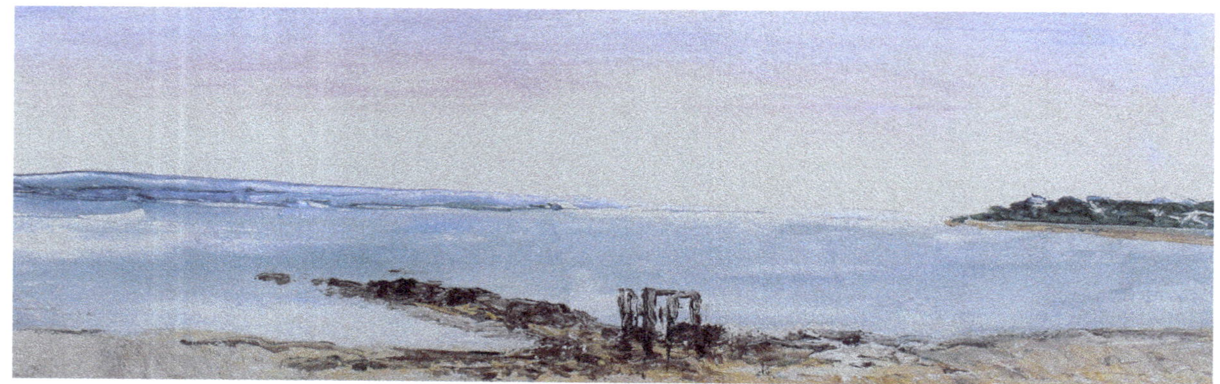

View like one would see in a wide angle camera lens.

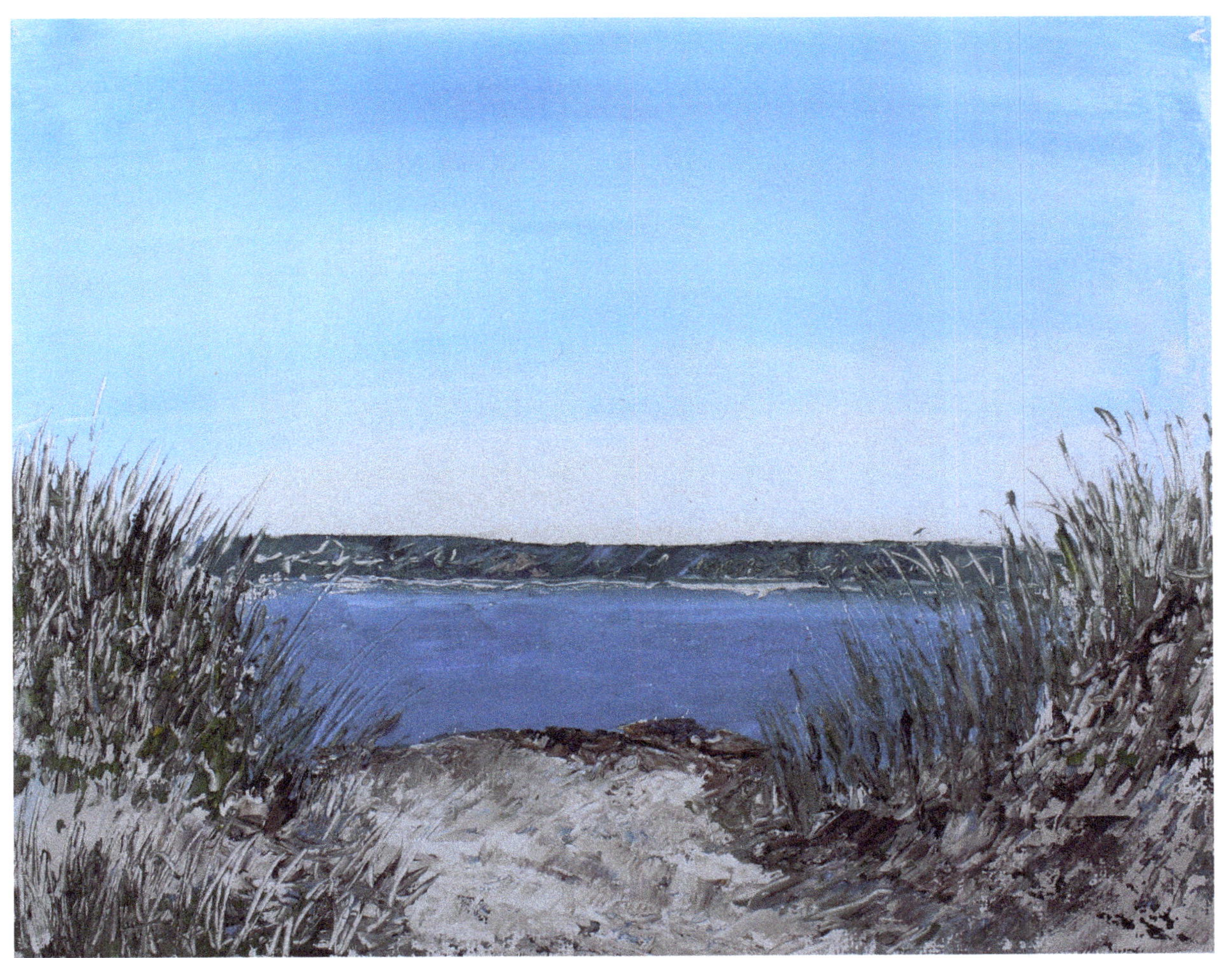

A different angle, from the east side parking lot, peeking through the dune grass to the beach. So much more fun to paint now that the grass is growing in and turning green.

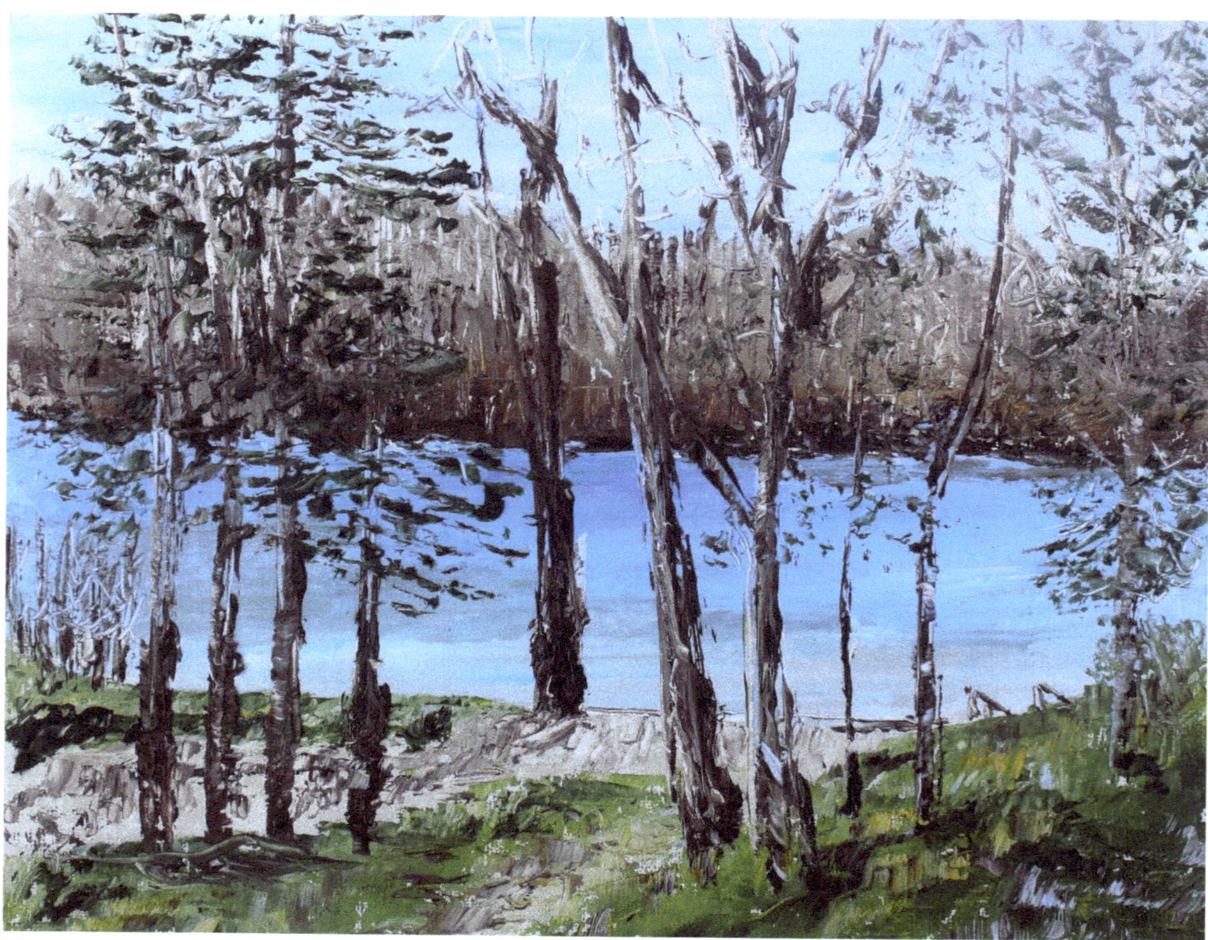

Went to Grew's Pond at Goodwill Park, even though I don't really consider it a 'beach." The Town of Falmouth does. I painted only one other there in the series, as I was waiting for things to turn green. The grass is now, though the trees (other than evergreens) are not. It was still beautiful, and a painting challenge to do the foreground trees. When painting with a palette knife, one relinquishes a lot of control. That's a good thing, because then the painting has more opportunity to surprise the one painting it!

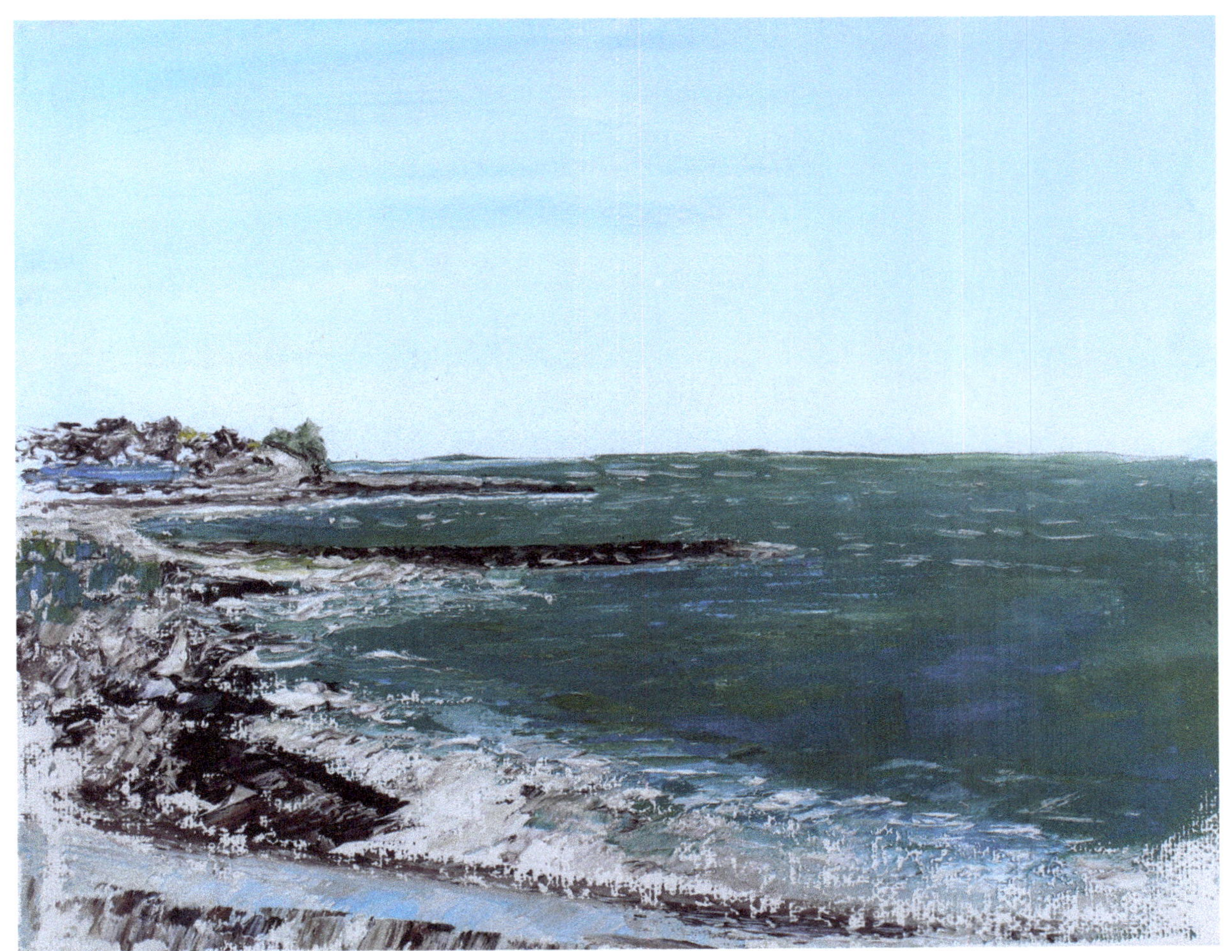

Also went to Surf Drive Beach, and did a second painting. What is it about a Dairy Queen sundae on a Friday afternoon that can feel like a mini- vacation? Thank you, Falmouth Dairy Queen, for the inspiration today.

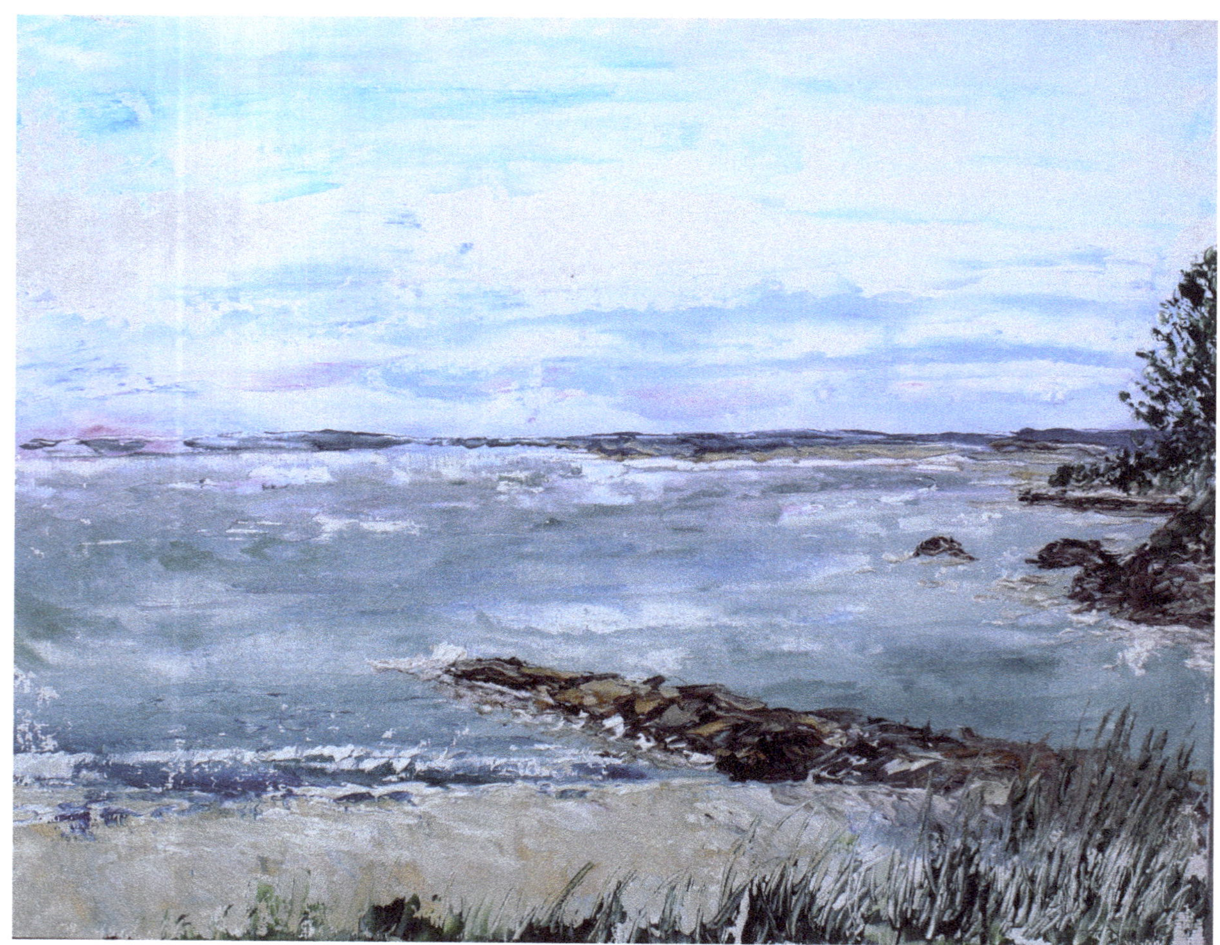

In the morning. Windy. Waves. Fun. Happy Mother's Day! Quick painting before church this morning. Then on the road after to meet halfway between the Cape and New York with my daughter and her fiancee for lunch. Our first fully vaccinated visit, after a year and a half of distancing. Oh, the hugs are so delicious!

DAY 39, MAY 9 - CHAPOQUOIT BEACH

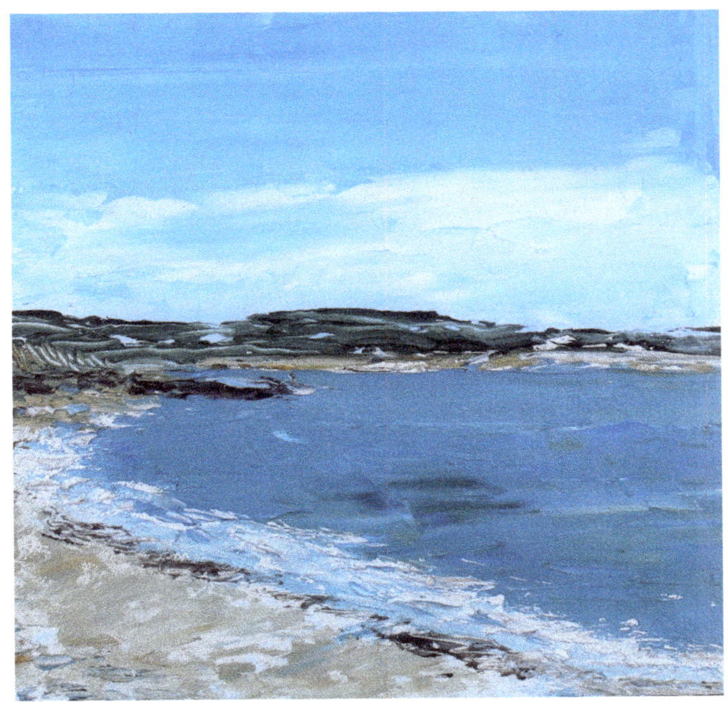

Blue skies. Beach of solitude.

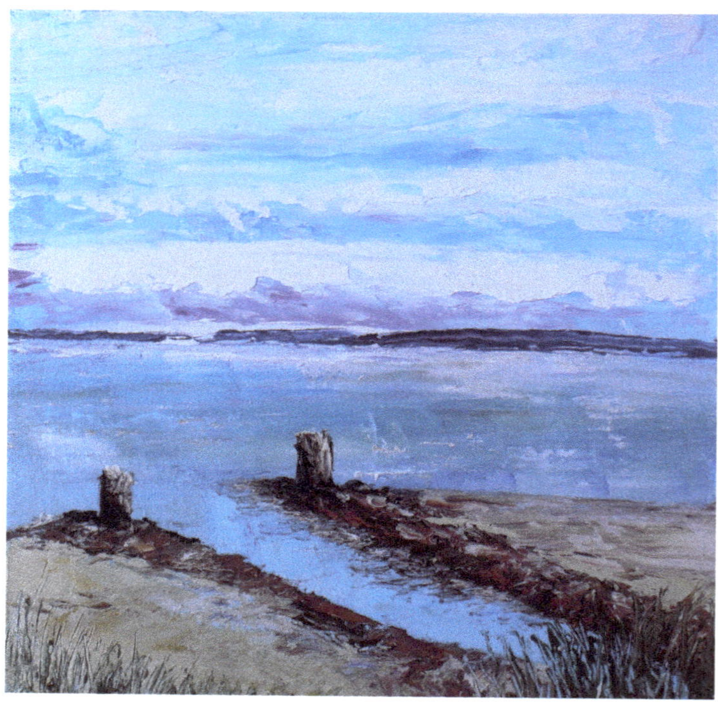

From the east side parking lot. Would you believe this was my first time looking at Menauhant from this side? Totally different view of the jetties.

DAY 41, MAY 11 - STONEY BEACH IN WOODS HOLE

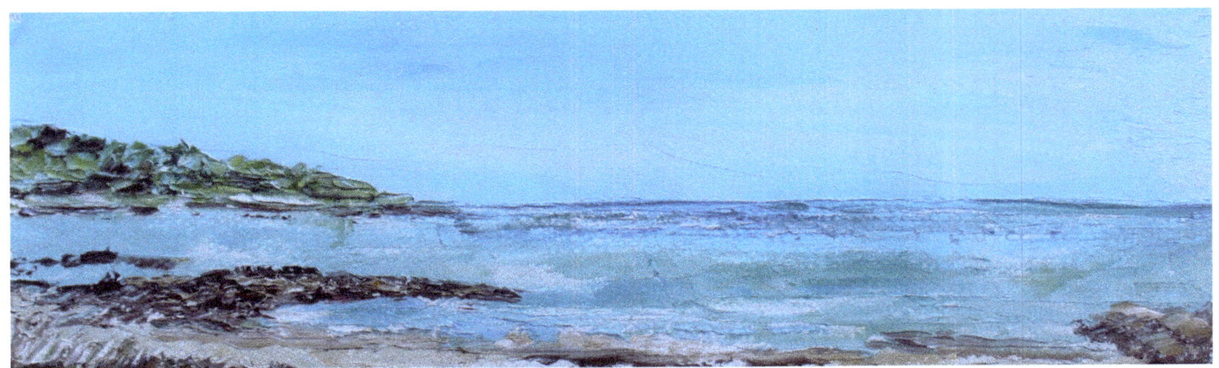

Beautiful sun today, and more wind.

DAY 42, MAY 12 - FALMOUTH HEIGHTS BEACH

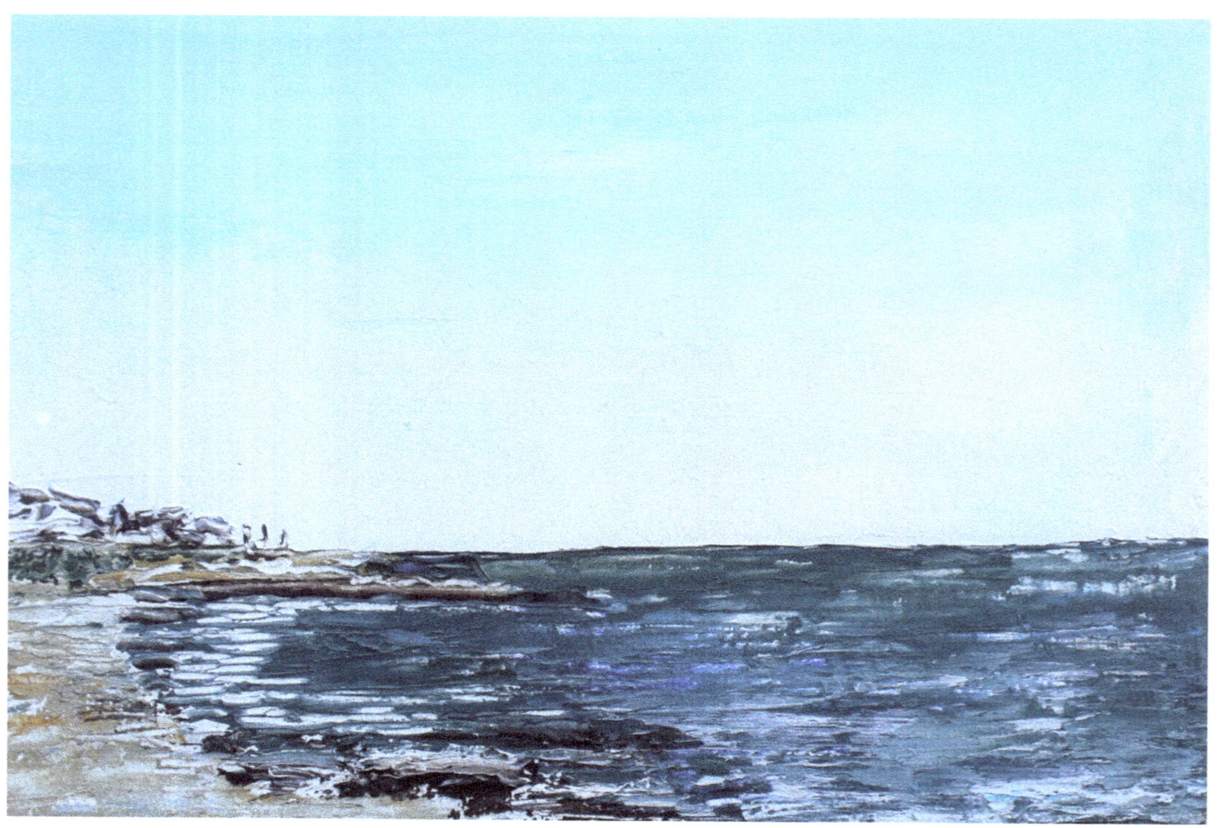

Two paintings, both at Falmouth Heights beach. Here is the first one.

DAY 42, MAY 12 - FALMOUTH HEIGHTS BEACH

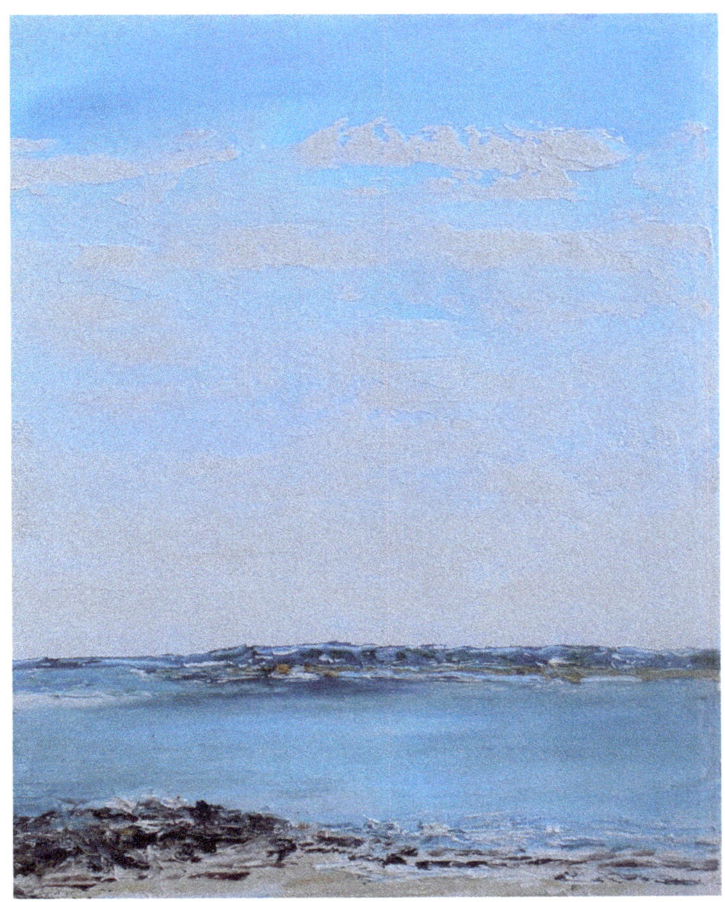

Here is the second one.

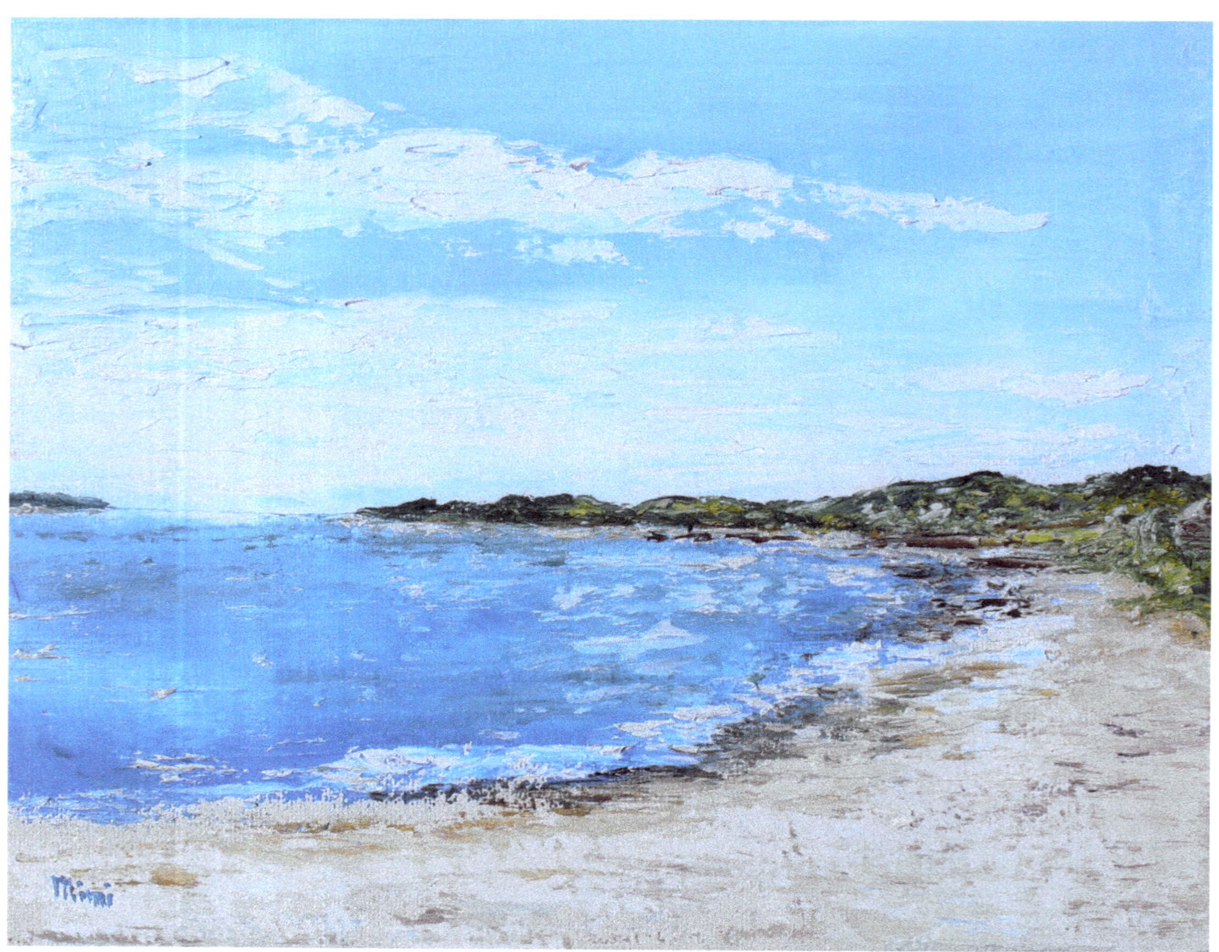

So fun to see the dune grass starting to come in, in a color so obviously named "spring green"!

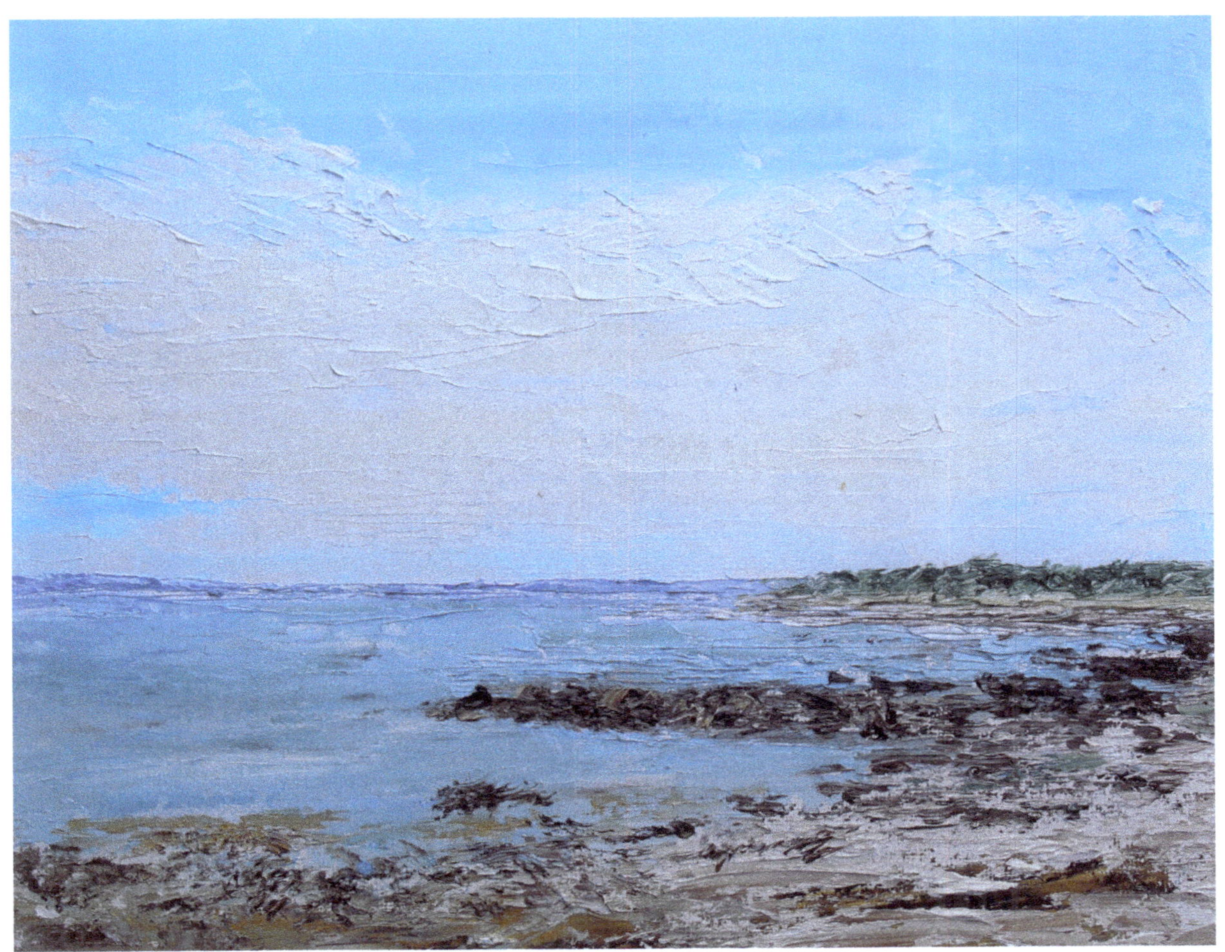

The one place where I must paint on the beach, not from my car, because there is no view from the car. Sooooo beautiful before the summer rush of visitors.

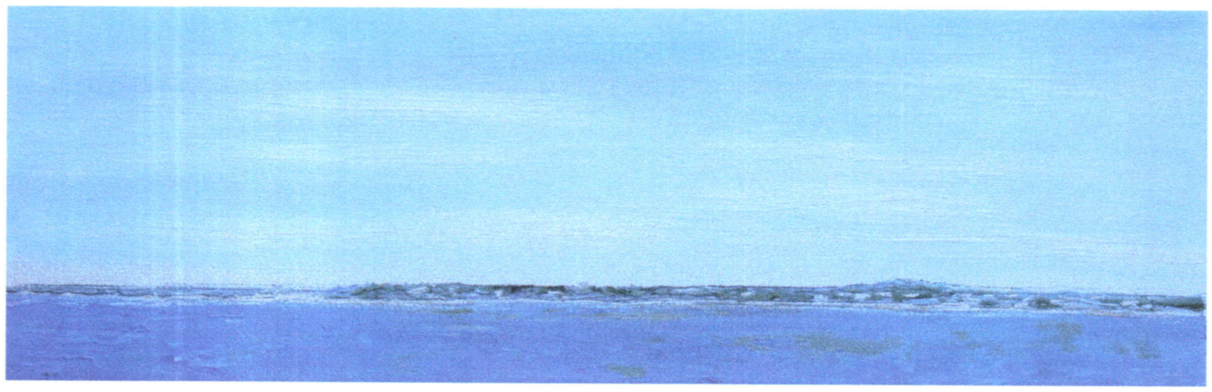

Early morning. Painted the sky with traditional paintbrush, and the water and land with palette knife. Just the water and sky, no beach or jetties on this one. It's what I see when I look across.

DAY 46, MAY 16 - CHAPOQUOIT BEACH

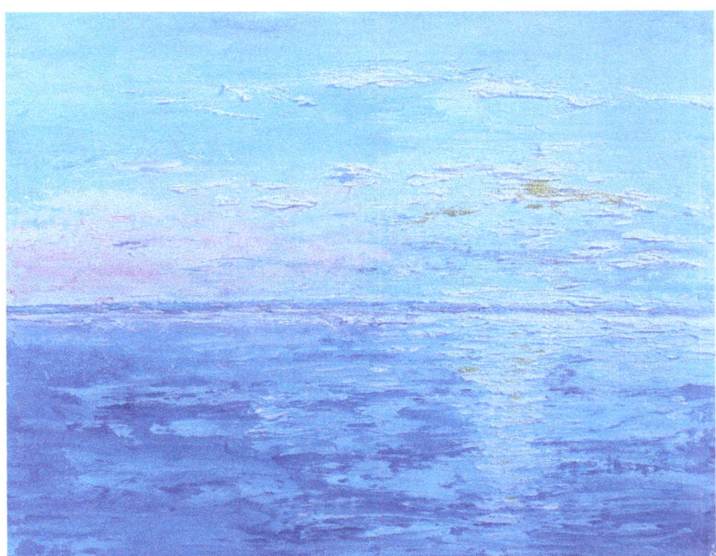

How could I do a series of Falmouth beach paintings and not include a Chapoquoit sunset? I used to paint a LOT of sunsets. This was the first in live time rather than from a photo, with a palette knife. Tricky. Colors and shapes constantly changing. And a challenge to capture the colors, as putting wet yellow paint into blue wet paint runs the risk of showing up as green in the sky (not a good thing.) Also, lost the light as the sunset progressed, so couldn't really see what I was painting! Had to capture a moment in time and go with it. Not sure what I think of the final result. What do YOU think?

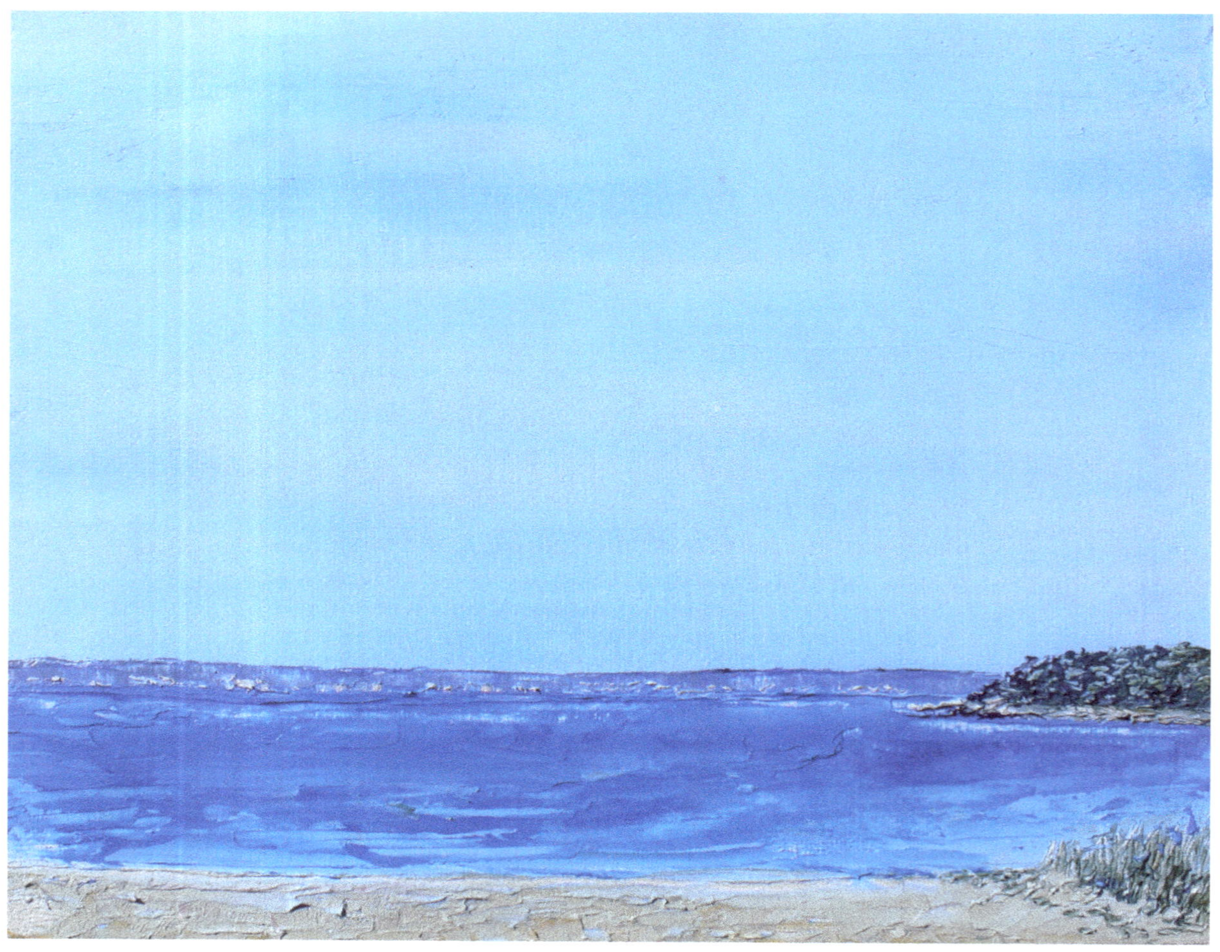

Relatively early this morning, before the clouds rolled in. Can you hear the song in my head? "Blue skies, nothing but blue skies..."

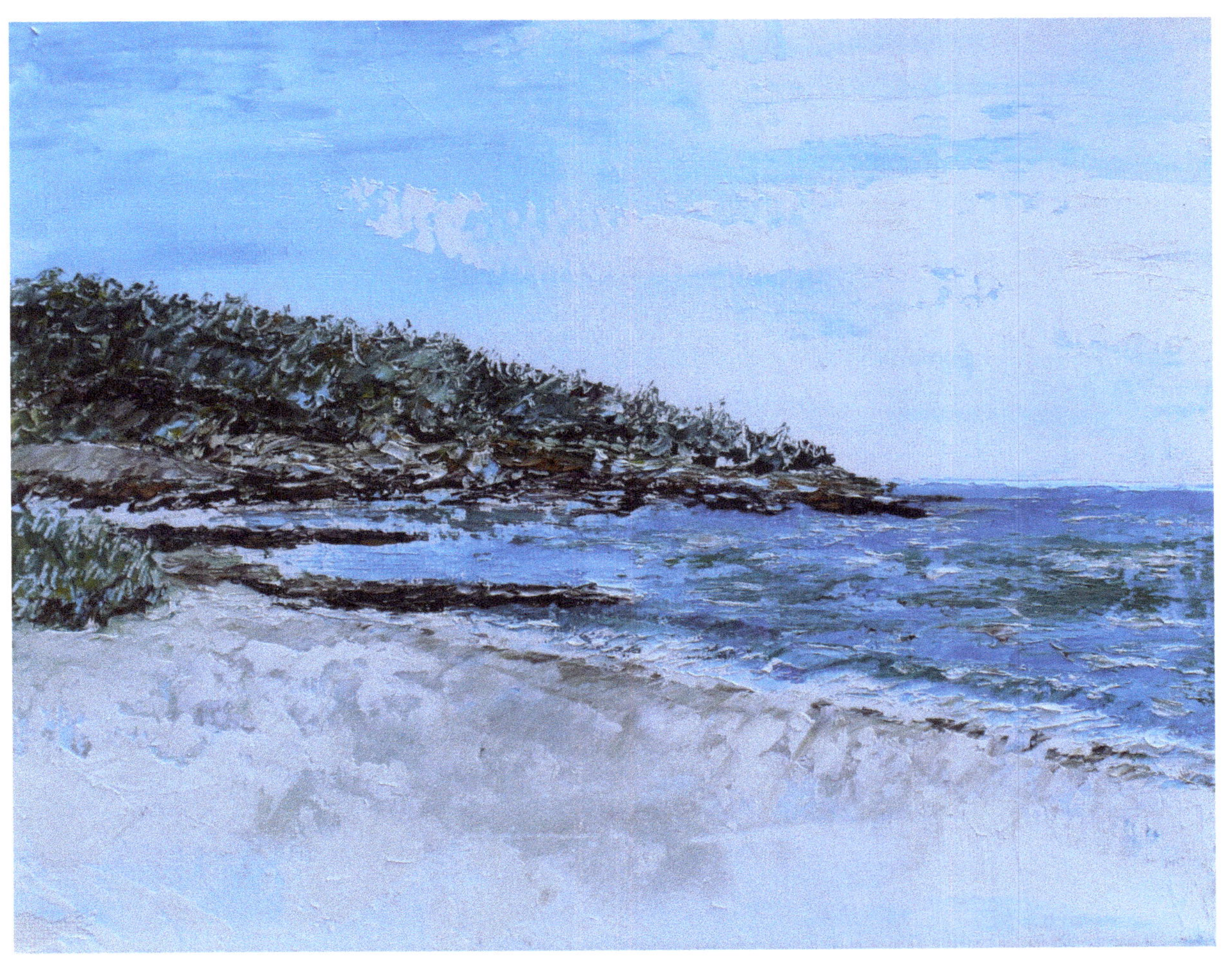

I'm often asked "how do you know when a painting is finished?" In this case, it was when the large pickup truck pulled into the space next to me and blocked my view!

DAY 49, MAY 19 - CHAPOQUOIT BEACH

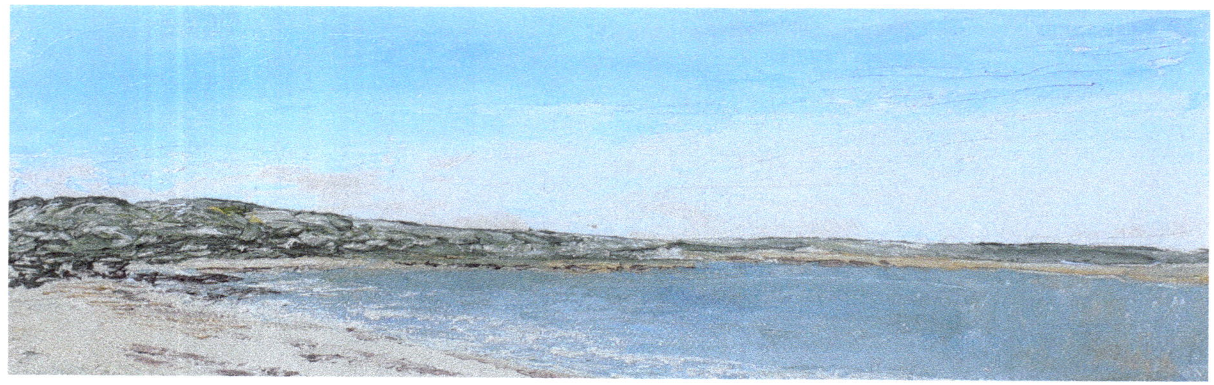

On a perfect weather morning in May. My goodness what a GORGEOUS stretch of weather blessing us this week!

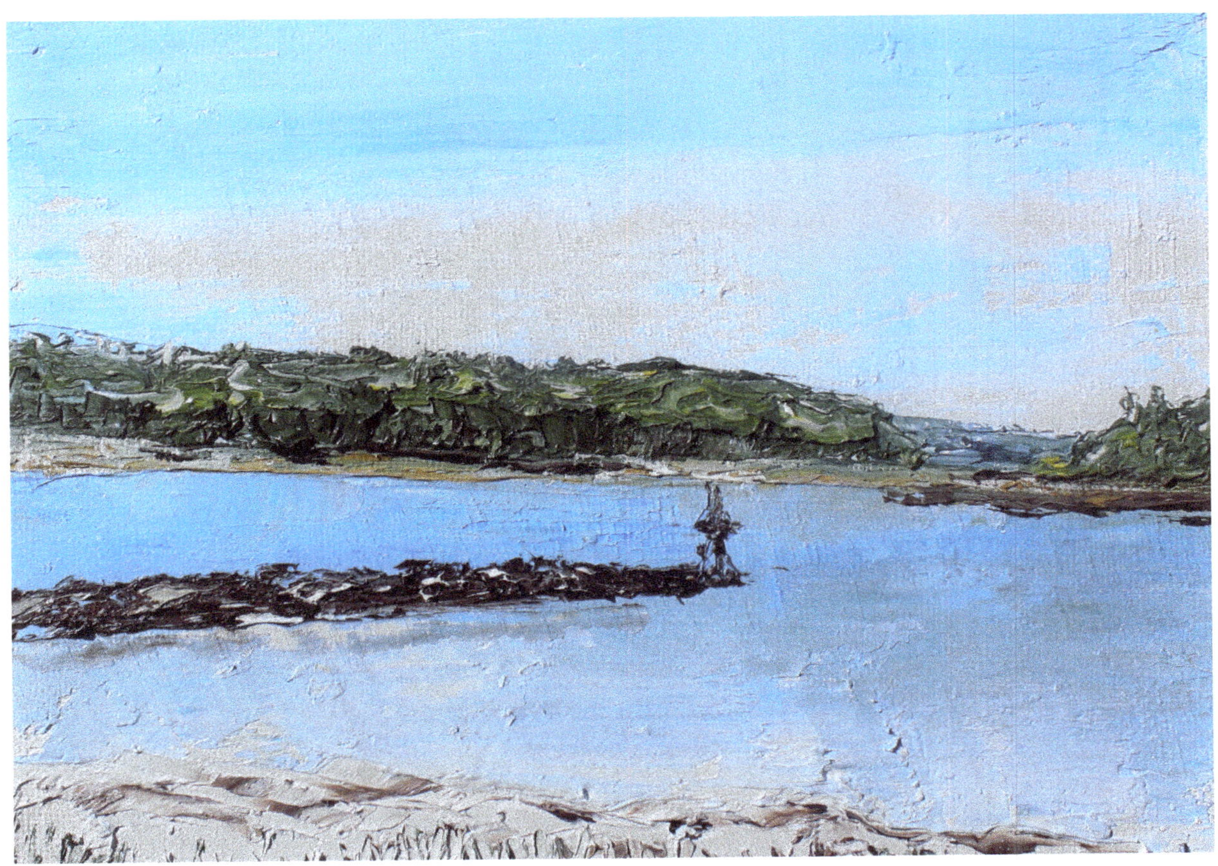

Megansett Beach, again, because, truthfully, my day got away from me, had a few emotional bumps in it, and I simply wanted to head to my happy place this afternoon.

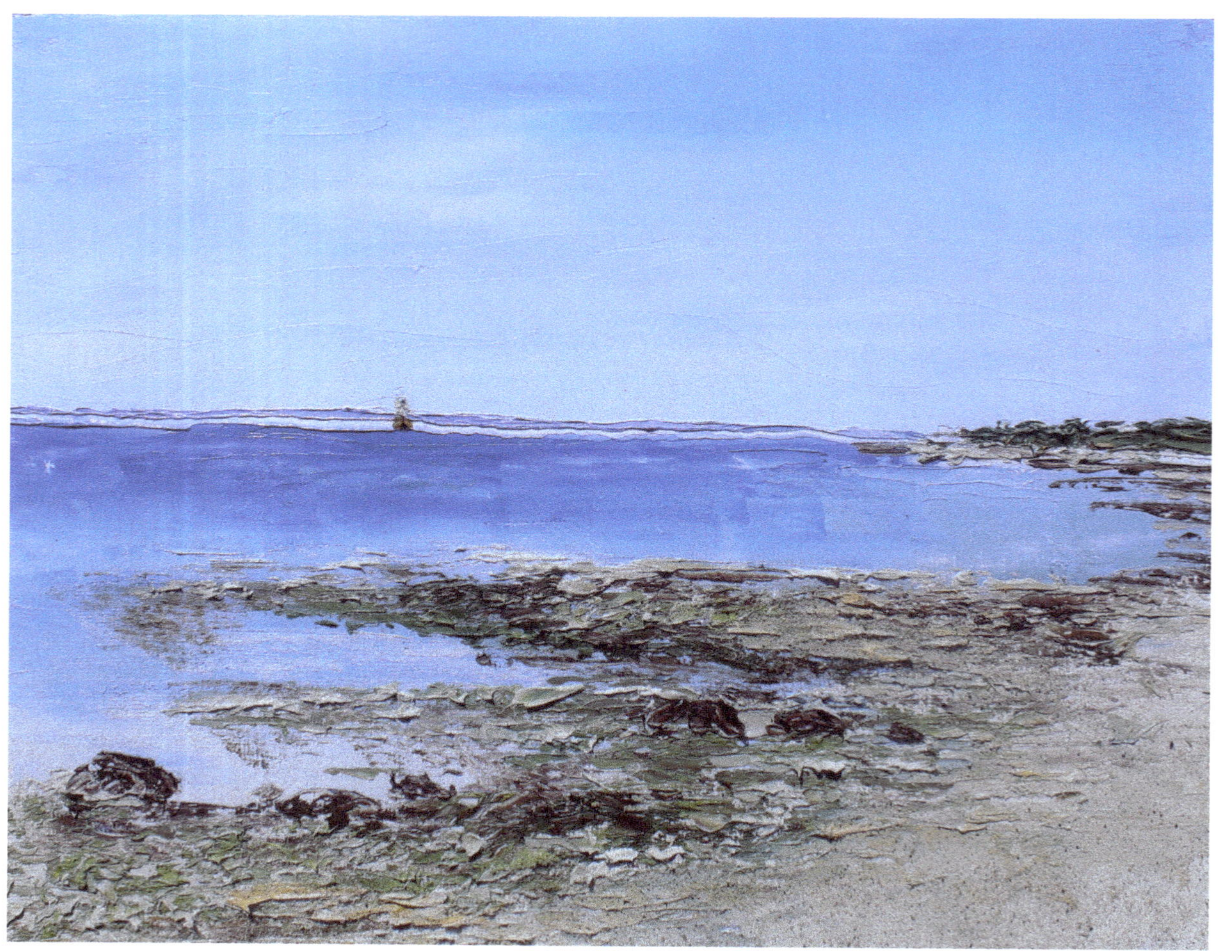

At low tide, it's sandbars and rocks. For fun and a hint of whimsy I sprinkled some sand into the wet paint on the beach part of the canvas. Extra texture, too.

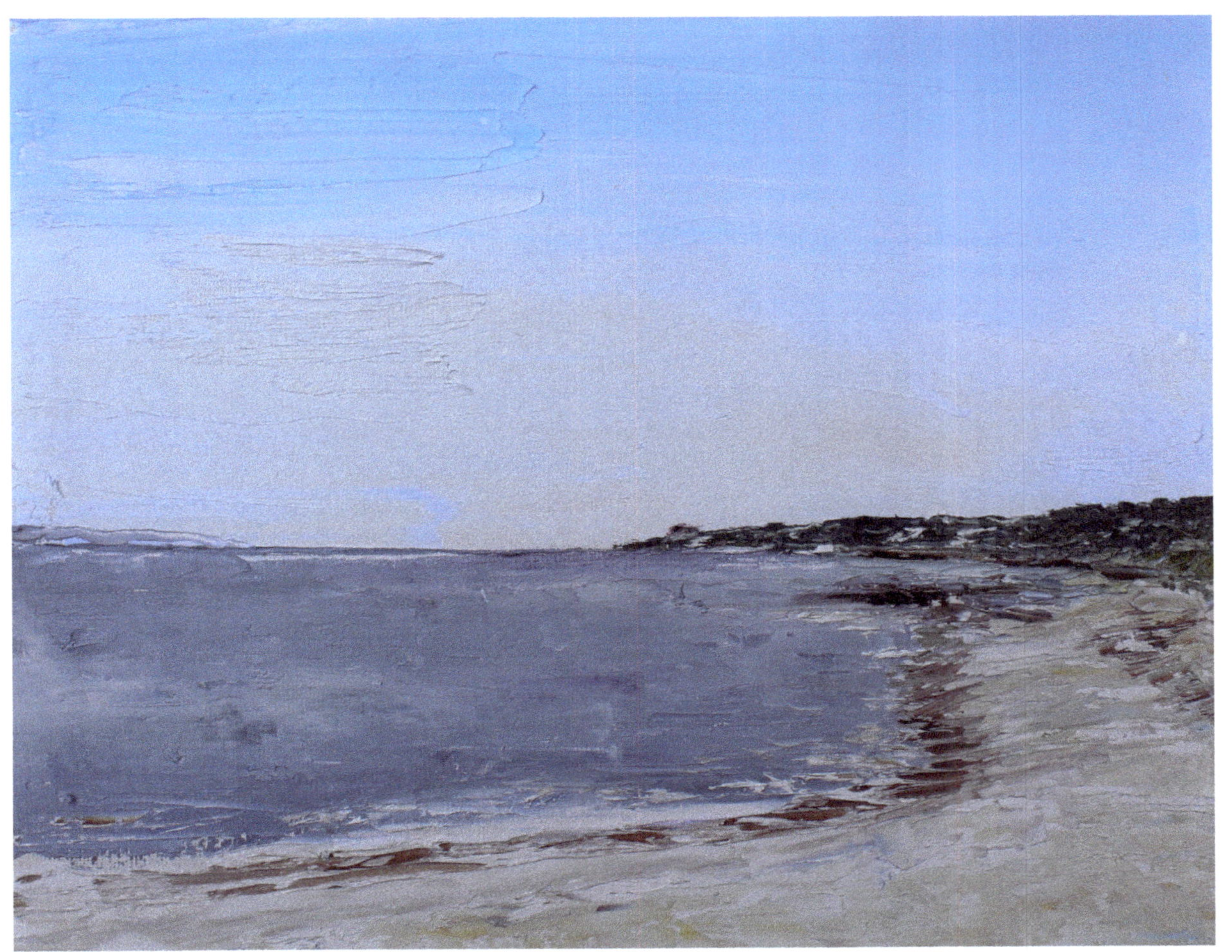

A lovely late afternoon. Two more to complete the project. Wondering where I should paint the final two.

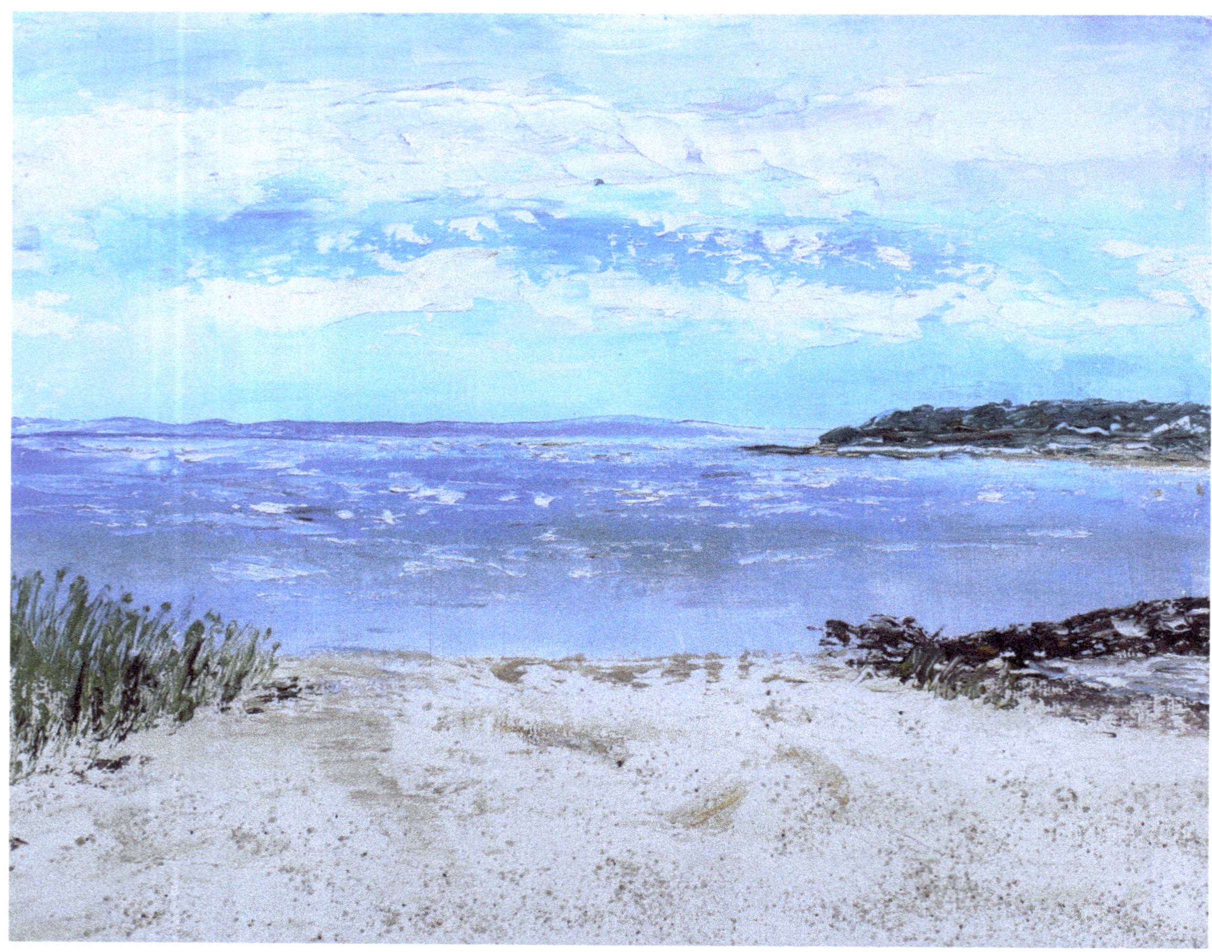

Watching the storm clouds roll in. There were a lot of people sitting on the beach. I chose to leave them out, for now. Sprinkled some sand in the wet paint of the foreground.

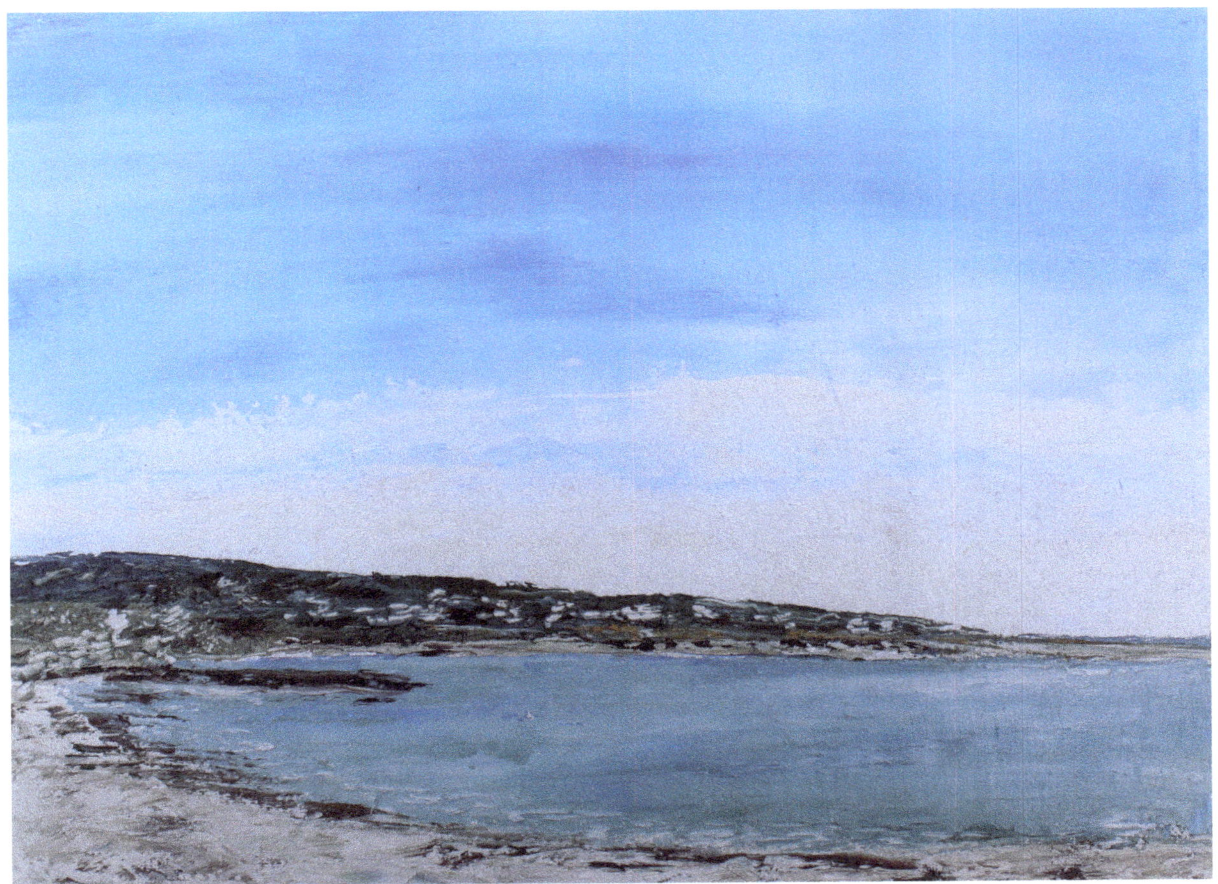

And.... that's a wrap. Chapoquoit Beach. Back to where it started on April 1. The project has been great fun, though I'm also, honestly, breathing a little sigh of relief at it being complete. Because there are many more fabulous Falmouth places to paint. Larger paintings, and commission paintings, waiting for me to get to them in my studio. Other mediums to explore . The front seat of a car to clean up. And a house to... well... don't even ask!

THE QR CODES

If QR codes are new to you... simply open the camera in your smart phone (or tablet) and hover over the code. Most will provide you right away with a link to a webpage. If not, you may need to download a reader app. Either way, they make this book interactive, leading you to YouTube videos of some of the painting days!

Day 7 Old Silver Beach   Day 8 Woodneck Beach   Day 9 Menauhant Beach

Day 16 Stoney Beach

Day 18 Bristol Beach

Day 19 Woodneck Beach

Day 23 - Chapoquoit Surf

Day 28 Woodneck Beach

All 54 paintings on MimisArt.com

THE OTHER 46

Day 55, the day when I should have rested and said, "Yay! I did 54! I can stop now."

Instead, my prevailing thought was, "54 is over halfway to 100, and people are loving these when I post them, and I love the painting time, so I might as well keep going."

So I did.

Now known as "The Other 46." Creative title, eh?

Enjoy.

Oh, and the new rule was that it didn't have to be a beach painting! The Other 46 is simply about painting an alla prima painting every day until day 100, July 9, 2021.

The images follow, along with captions about some of the new things I learned along the way. They continue to be done in one sitting, on location, with no refinement in the studio. So be warned, a few of them were a bit experimental and perhaps even a little embarrassing to me to publish, but I'm being true to the project.

One new painting, every day, posted "as is" with the accompanying social media post comment.

Enjoy!

DAY 55, MAY 25 - WEST FALMOUTH INNER HARBOR

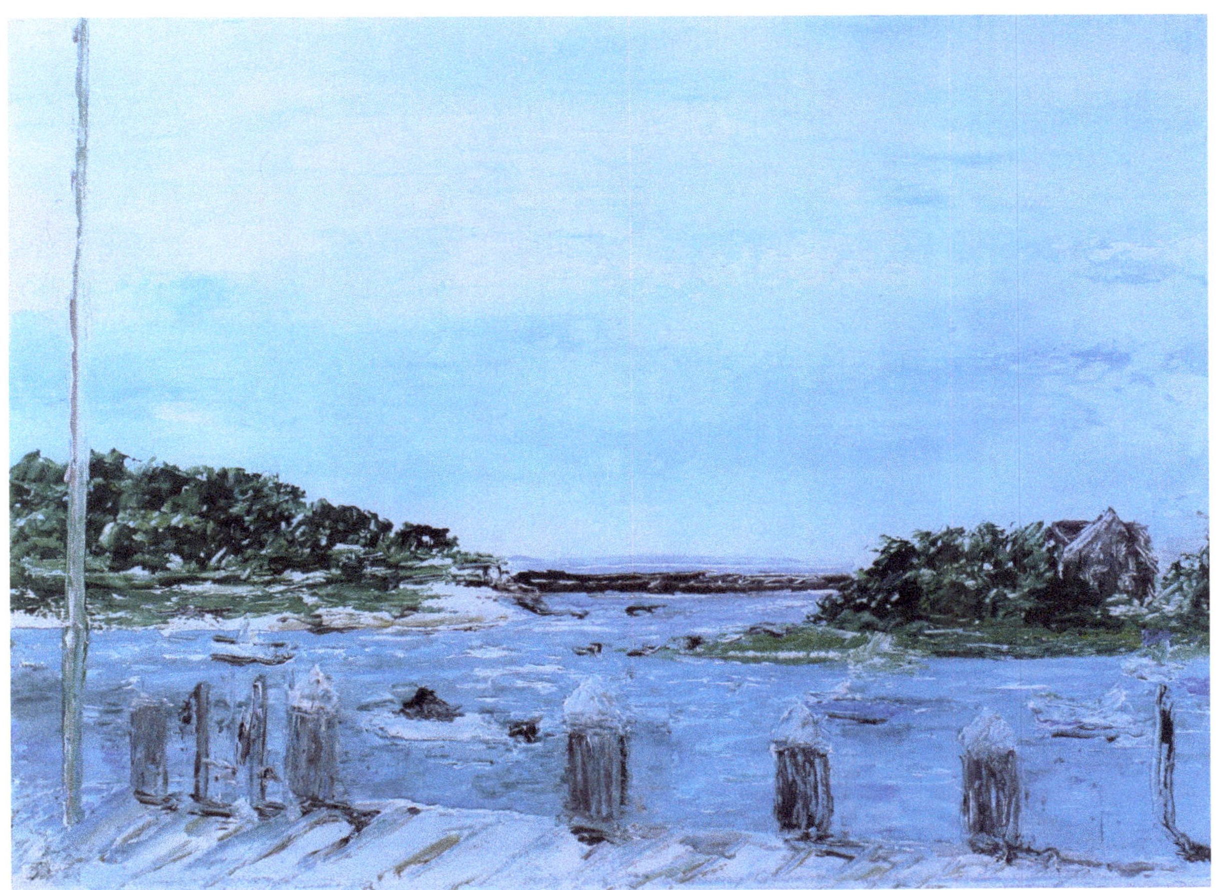

I sat by the boat dock at West Falmouth Harbor. Now I must say, doing that scene, with a lot more detail in front of me than the beaches, was a significant challenge in oils and palette knife. Not sure how I feel about the result, but sharing it anyway. I invite you to enjoy it simply for what it is. Thanks again everyone for your ongoing support and encouragement!

DAY 56, MAY 26 - CHAPOQUOIT BEACH FOG

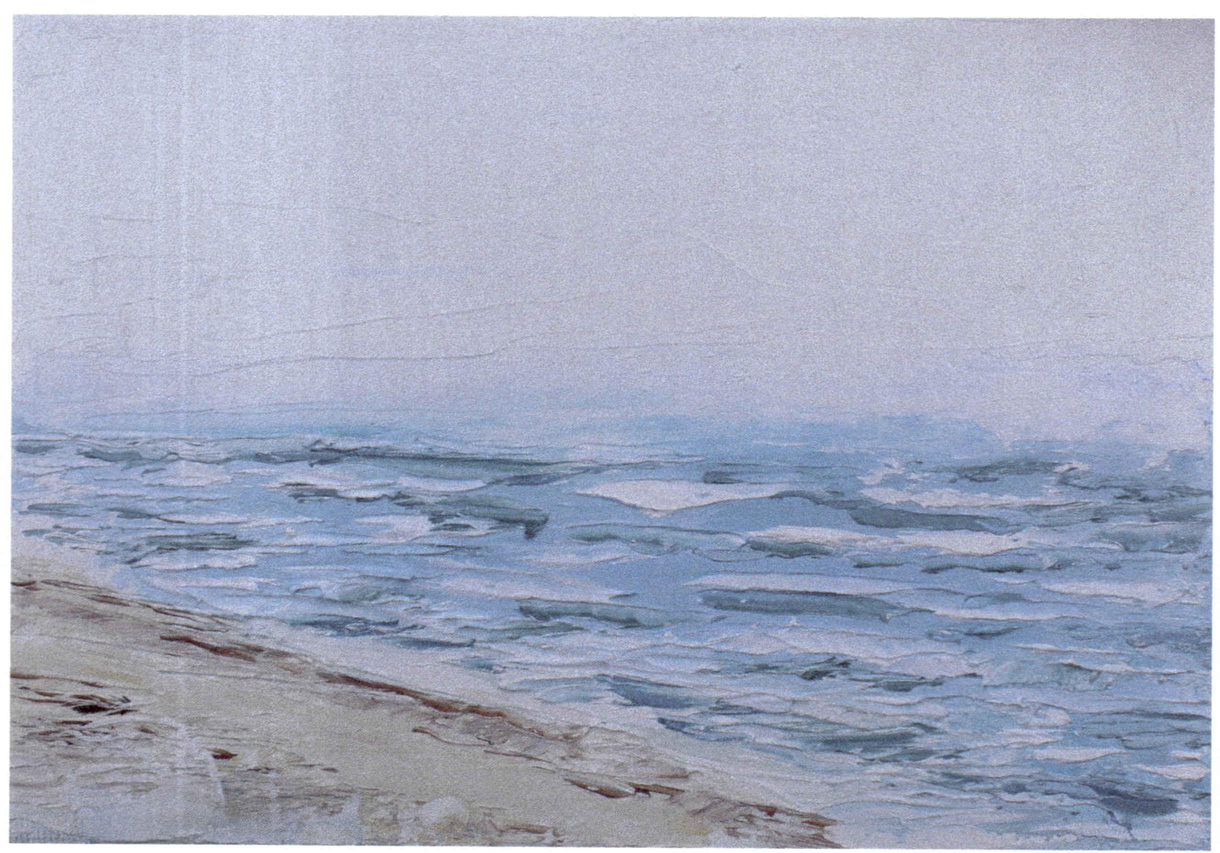

FOG! So dense, there was no horizon line, only a blur in the distance. And surf and whitecaps. Made for a pretty fun impressionistic painting. While this was at Chapoquoit, it really could be just about anywhere. Enjoy.

DAY 57, MAY 27 - ROSA RUGOSA - BEACH ROSES ALONG SURF DRIVE

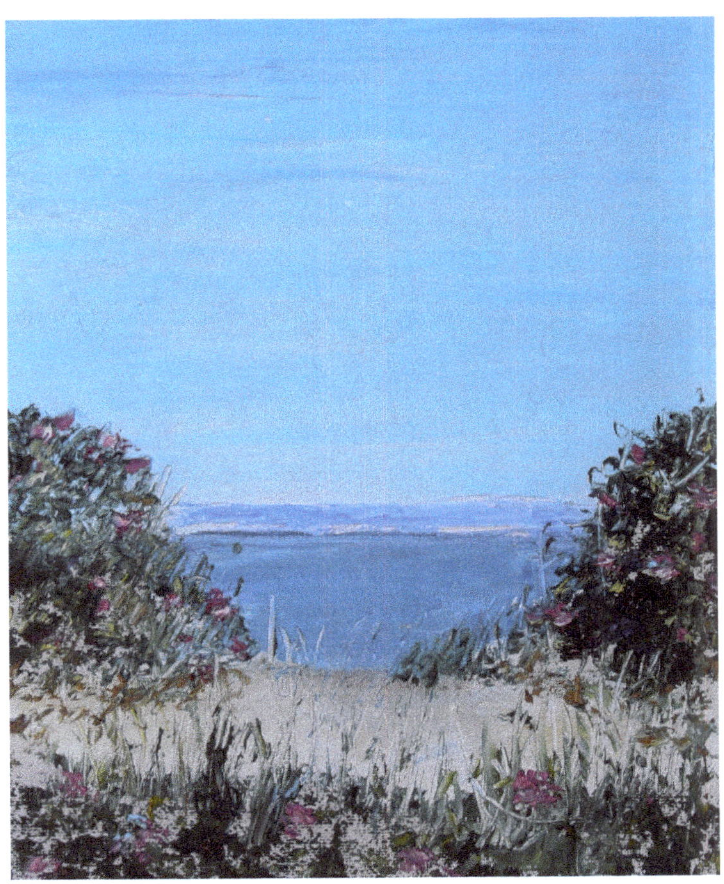

Rosa Rugosa (beach roses) along Surf Drive. Must be almost summer! Enjoy.

DAY 58, MAY 28 - BACKYARD LILACS

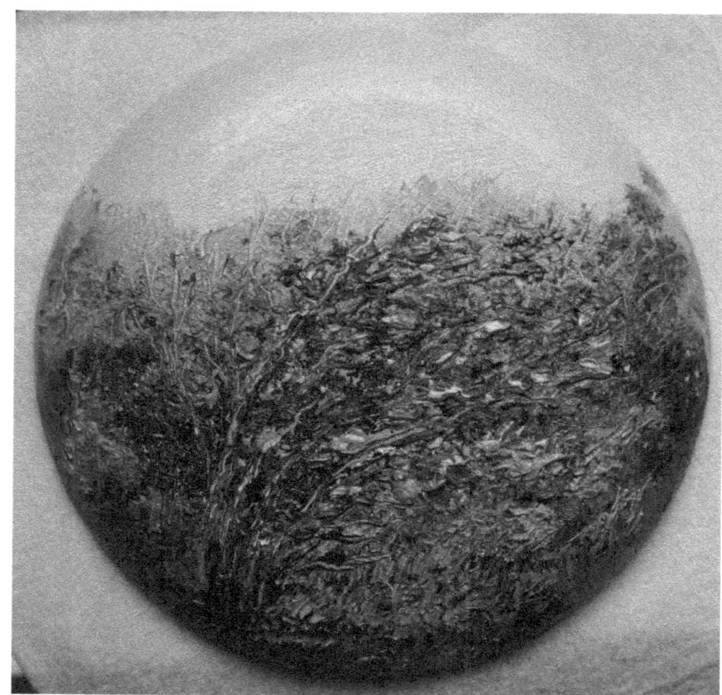

Something very different today. A lilac tree in my backyard. Lost the light as rain started. The canvas is called "convexo." It is 8" round, with a beveled edge.

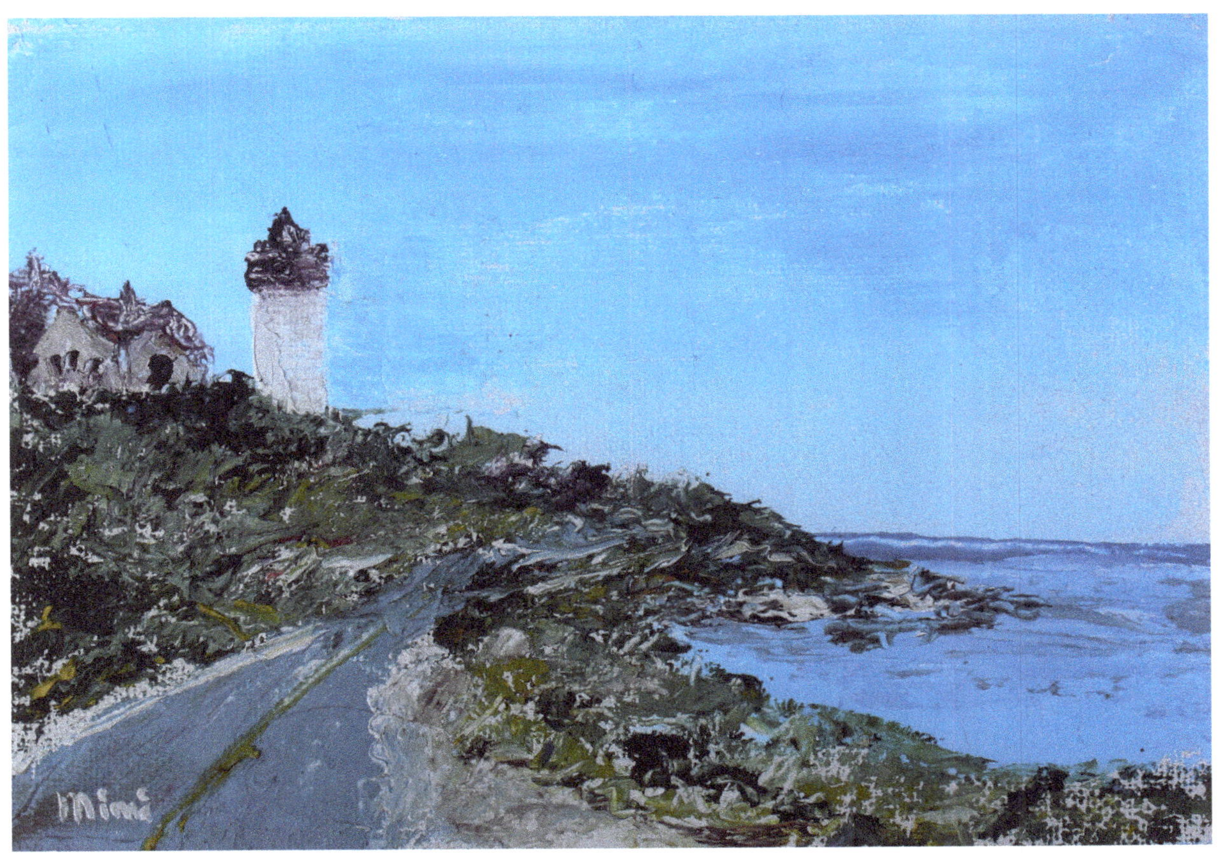

Headed down to Nobska earlier this morning, in the rain. Quick little improvisation Happy weekend! Gotta love 46 degrees and raining on Saturday of Memorial Day weekend!

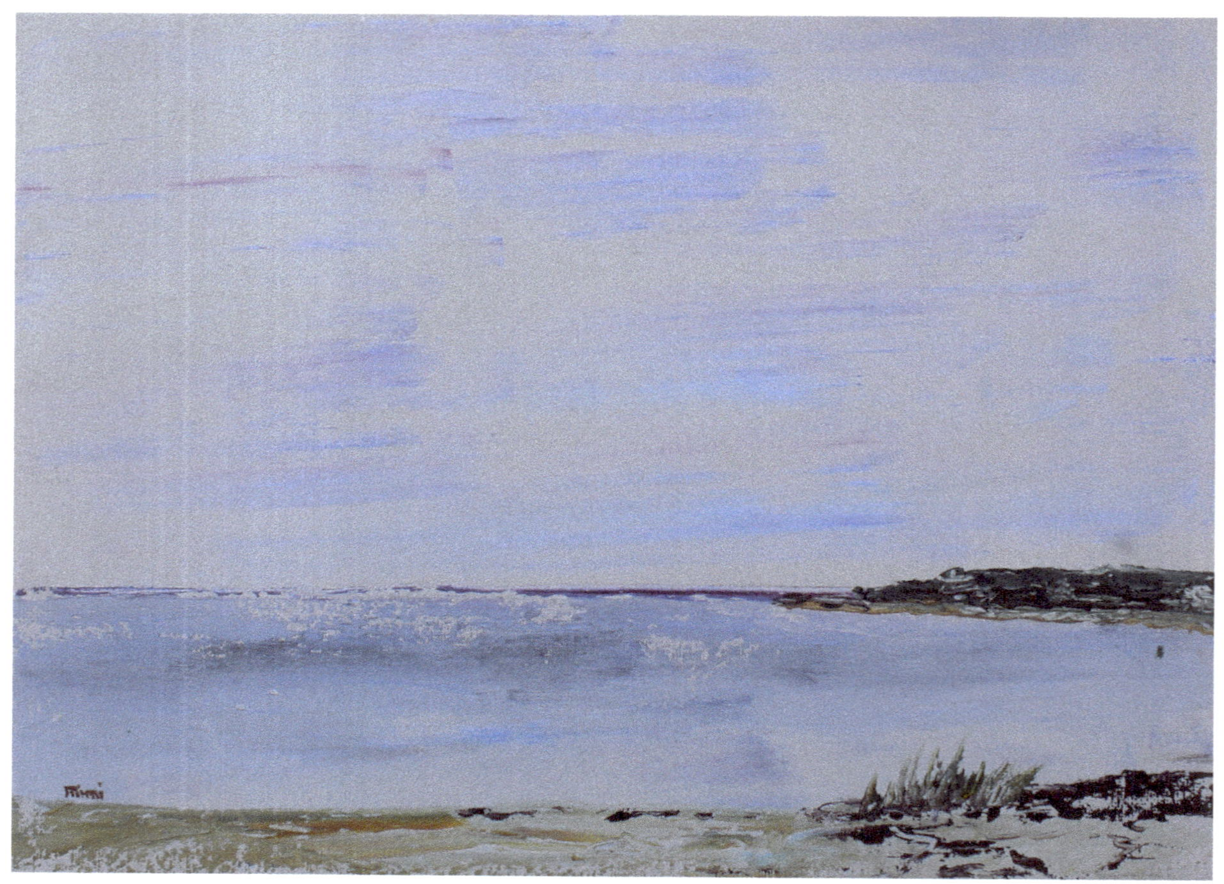

Stopped at Megansett on way home from church.

DAY 61, MAY 31 - CHAPOQUOIT BEACH IN FOG

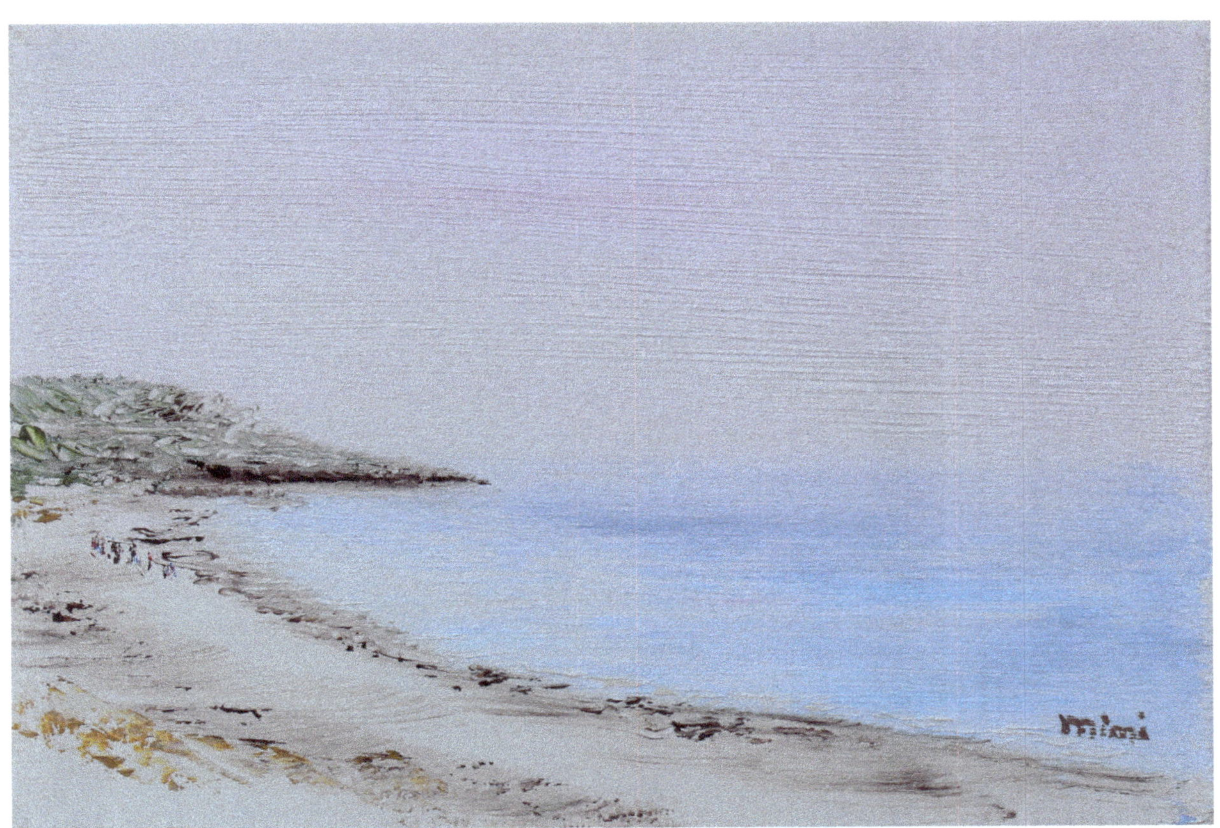

Went to Chapoquoit Beach this morning while fog was still dense. Makes for a minimalist small oil painting. A few people walking on the beach in the distance.

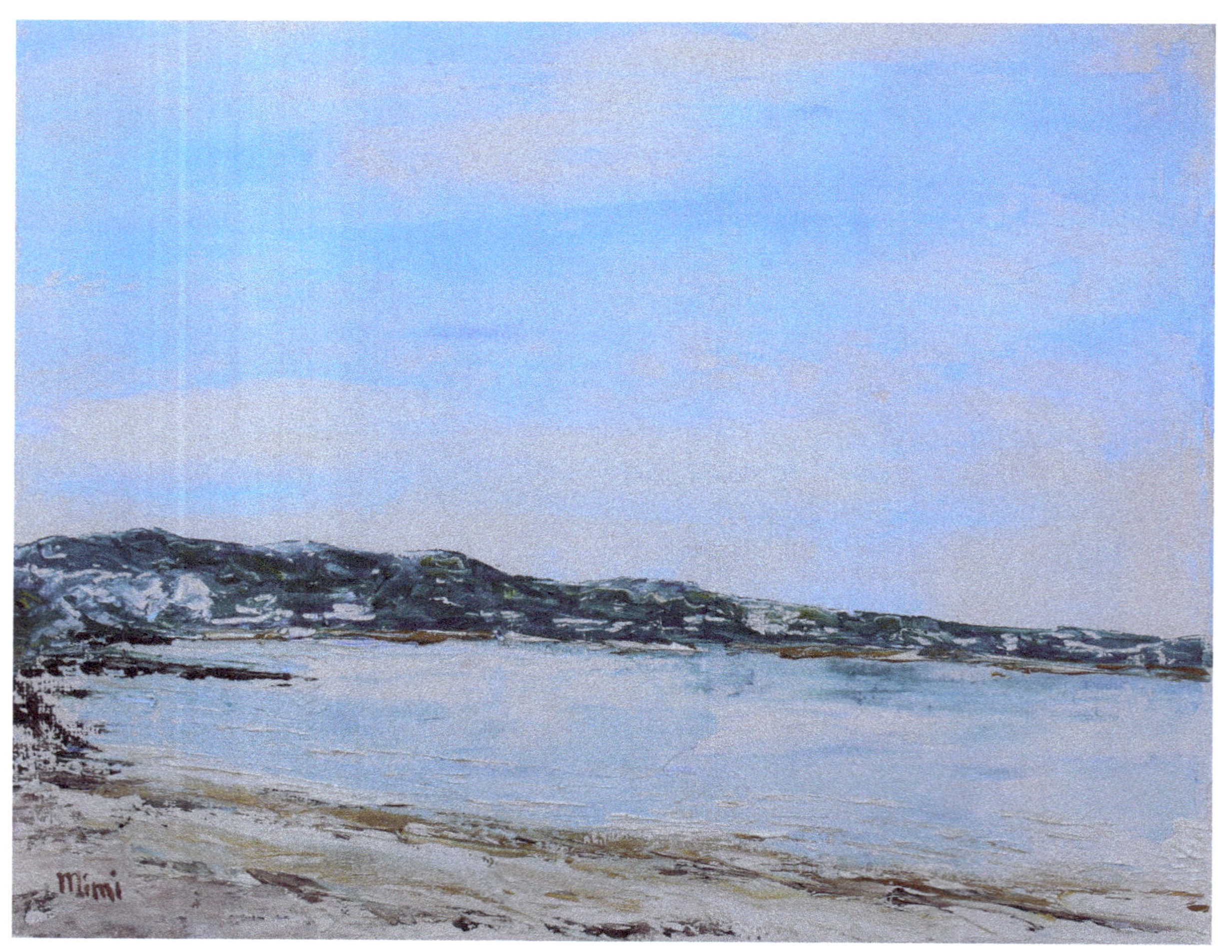

Chapoquoit Beach. Keeps drawing me. And I keep drawing it!

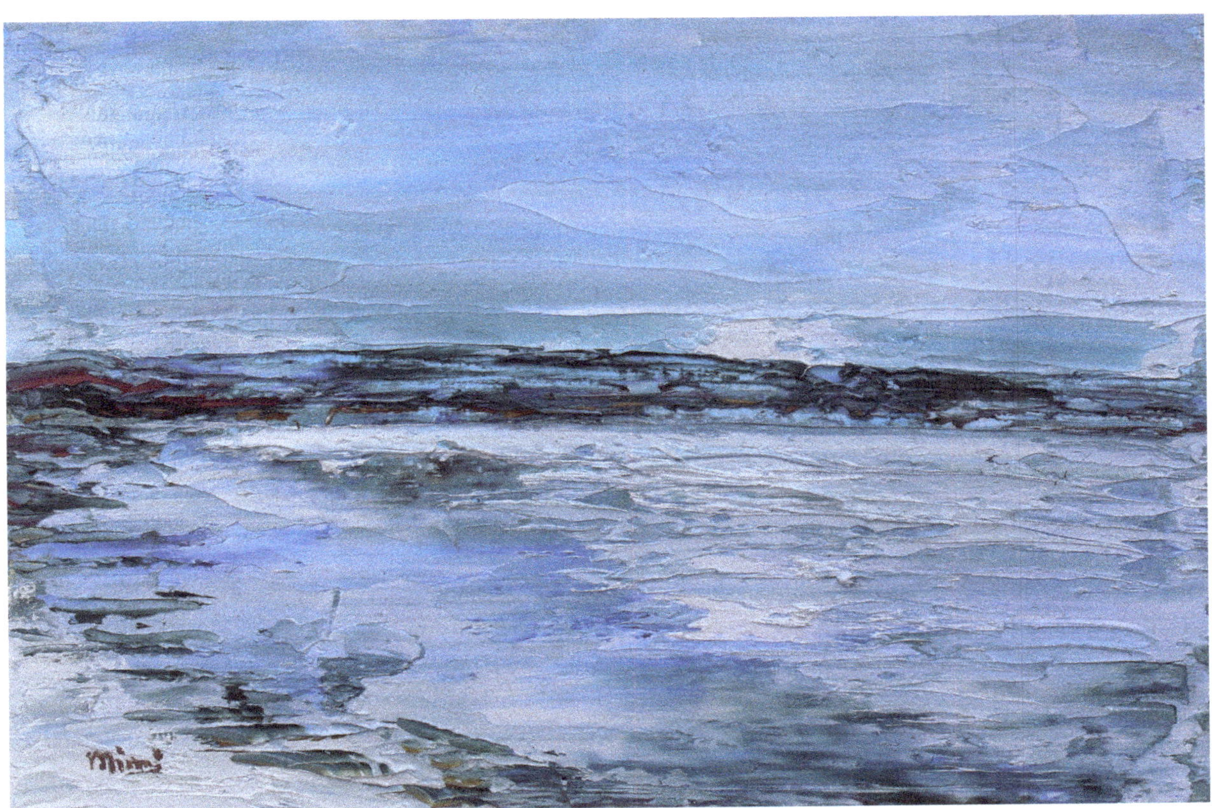

It was bound to happen eventually, after 63 days of posting a new painting online every day. Decided to challenge myself today to learn how to do scenes with architecture using the painting knife. Epic fail! So frustrated that about halfway through I took the palette knife and smeared the entire painting out smooth, real thick. THEN, sitting there in my car on the village green, painted from my head a sky over water scene using the same paint that was smeared on the canvas. So it's a bit greener sky and water than usual.

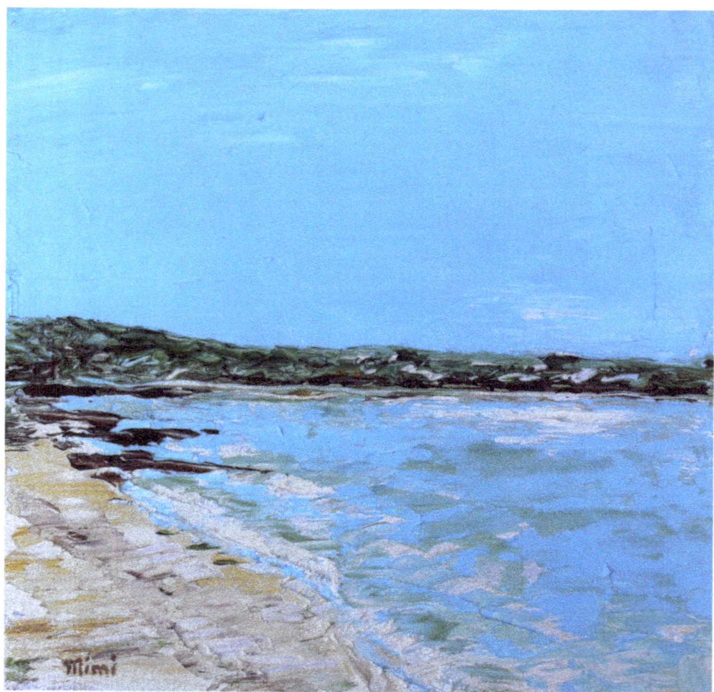

Feeling too sunny on the inside today to paint the fog outside. So I parked at
Chapoquoit then made up my own colors!

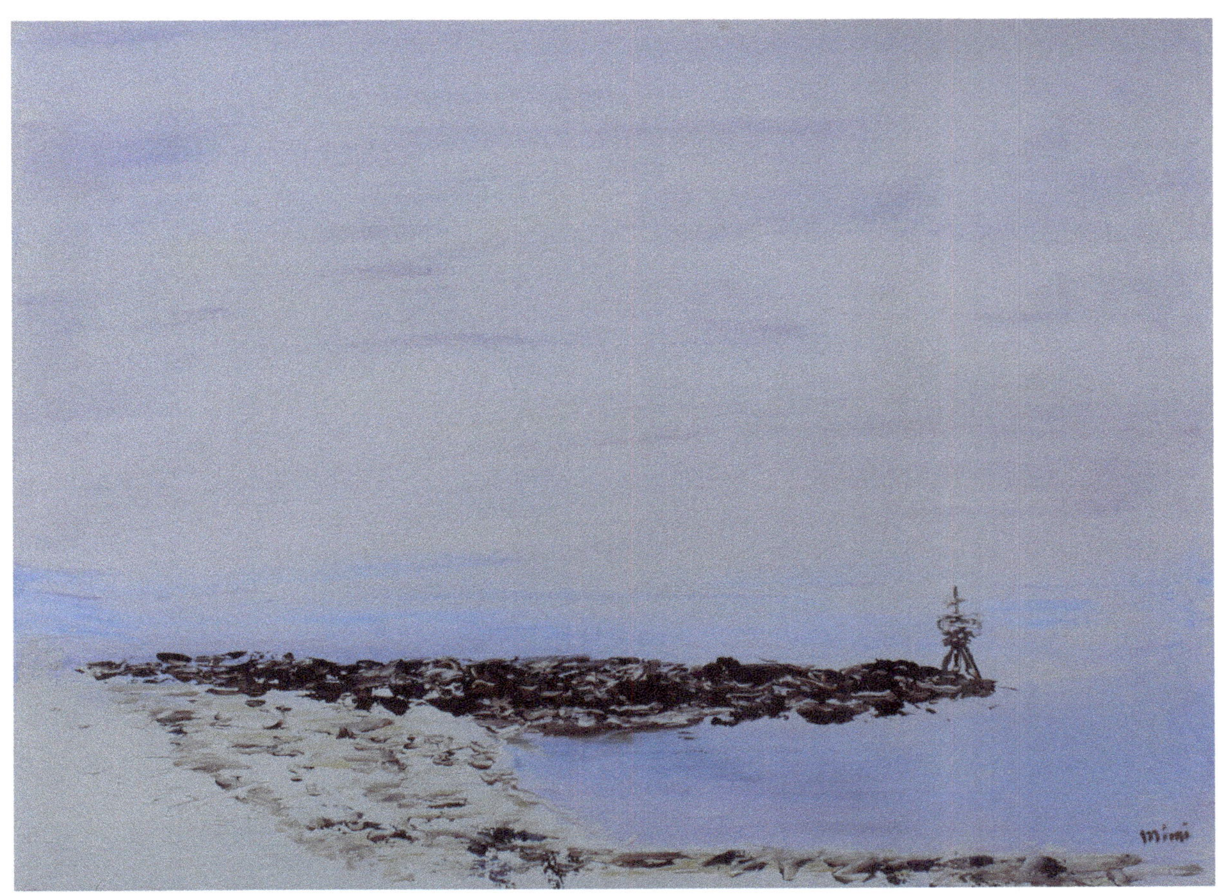

Megansett Harbor jetty in the dense morning fog.

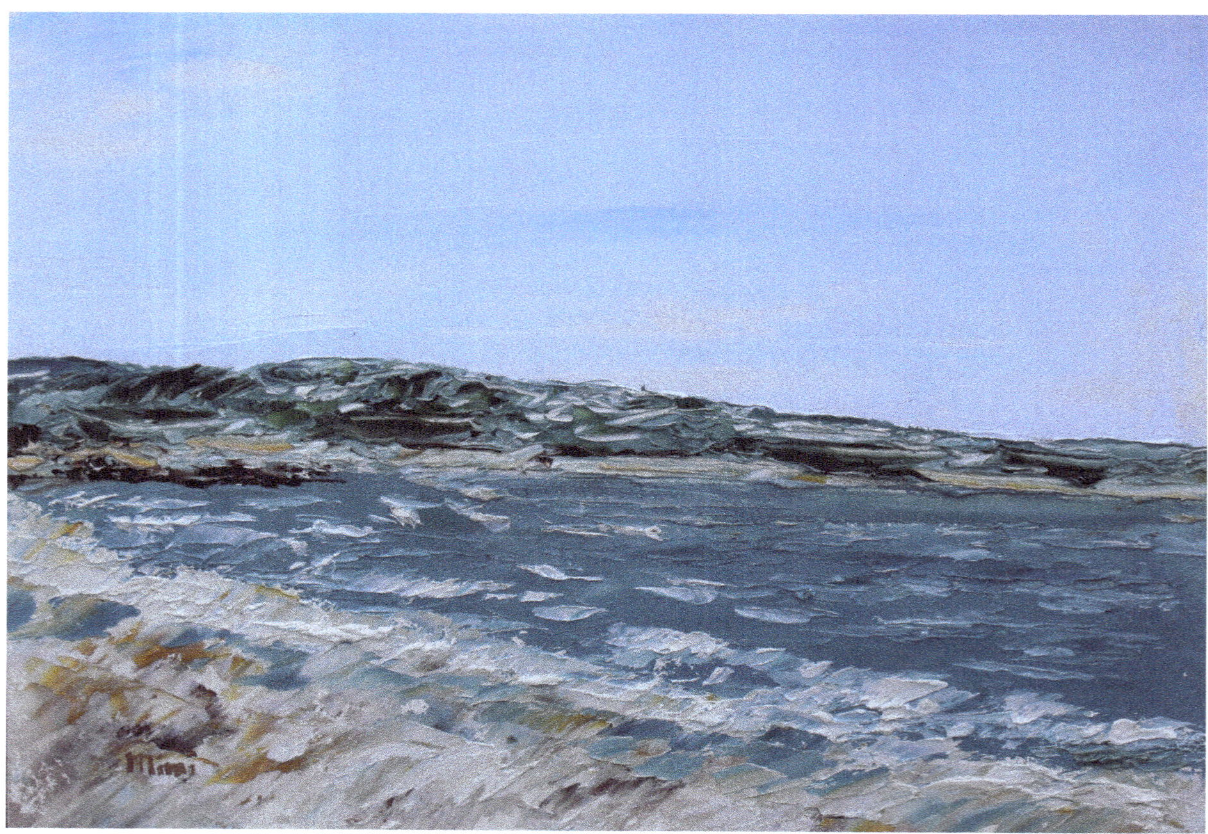

Chapoquoit Beach. Yes, there were people on the beach. No, I did not include them. I live here year round. I'm spoiled. Accustomed to the peace and quiet of an empty beach on a cold, windy day. Takes a little getting used to... that there are others around! So for now, I leave them out of the picture. Been a year of embracing my inner introvert. I need to ease back into crowds. Enjoy the sunshine everyone. We are MEANT to share it, not to live in isolation. Love one another. Smile with your full face. Brighten someone else's day. Everyone has a backstory. You never know what a simple smile, or an extra thank you, can do.

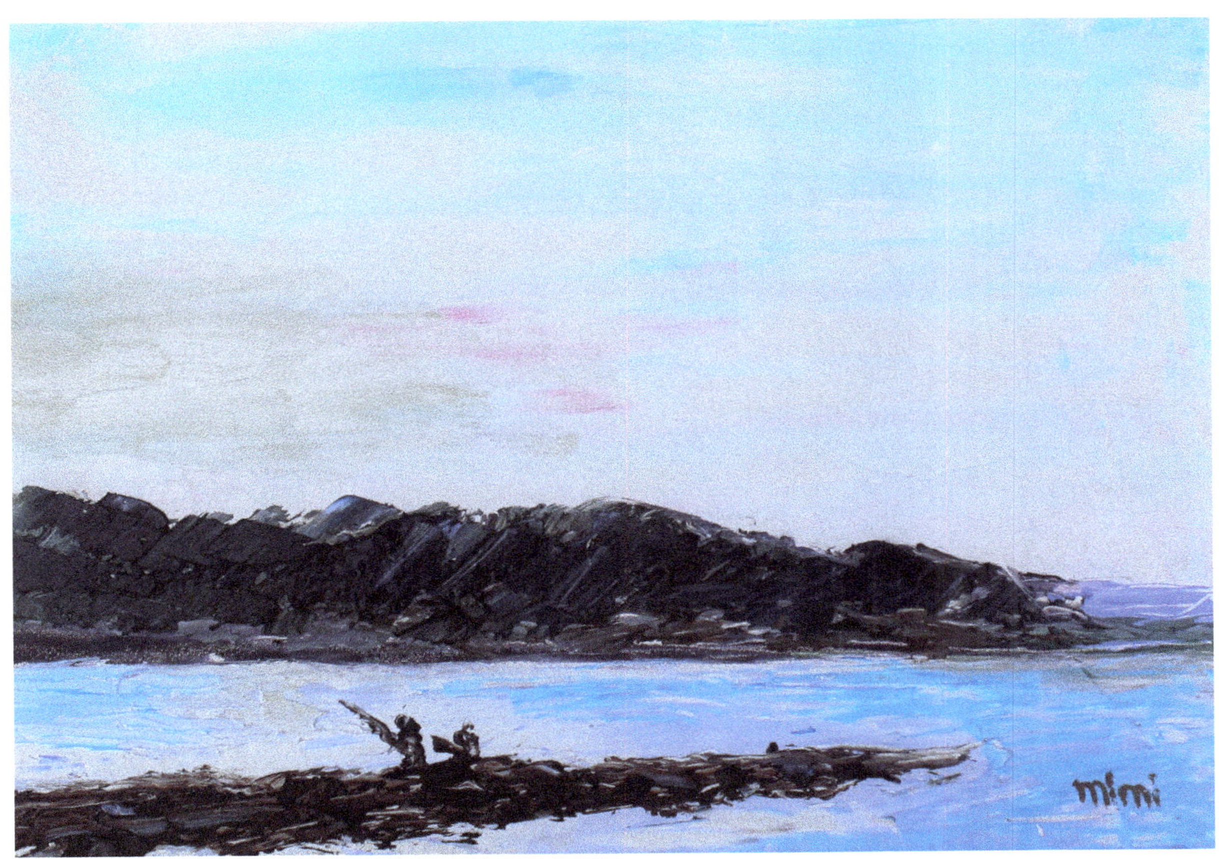

Dusk. All becomes silhouette, even those fishing on the jetty.

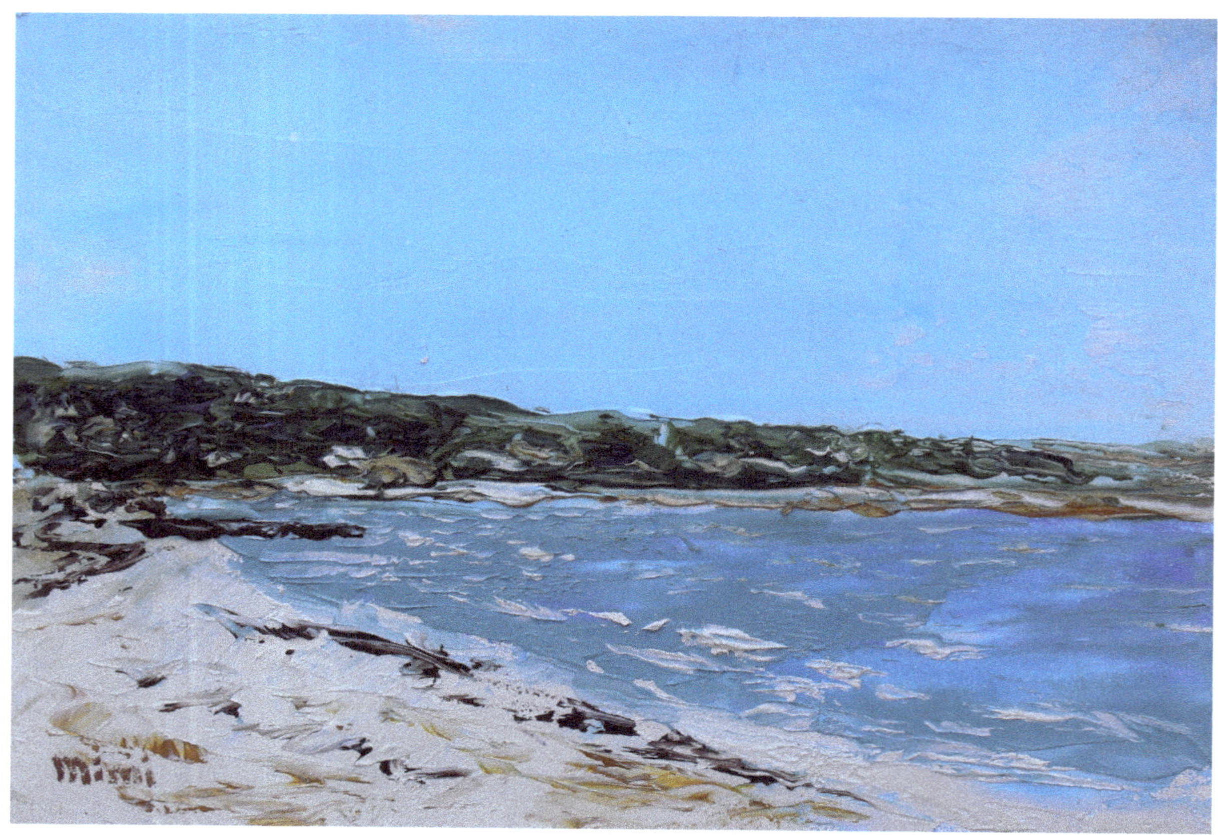

Chapoquoit beach before the fog rolled in. Happy Monday!

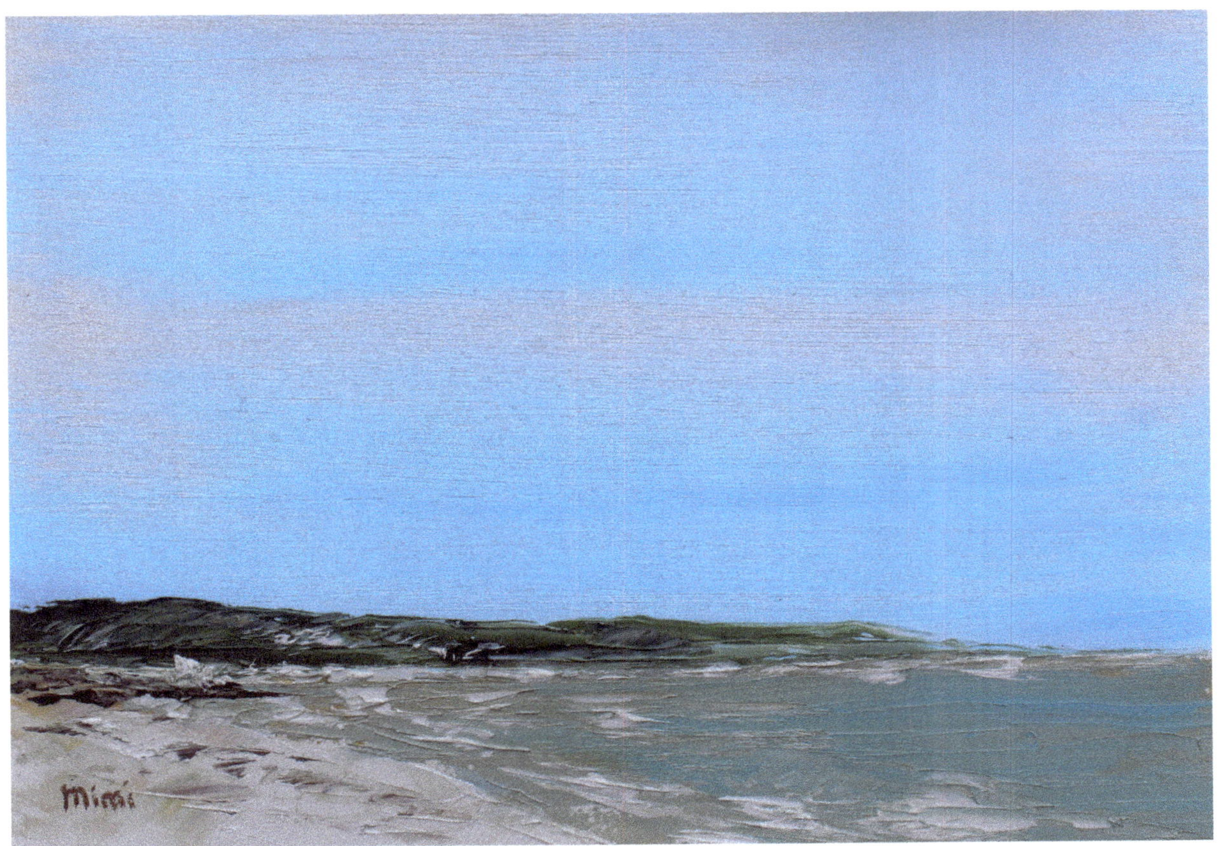

A second one today, because I'd rather paint than tackle the pile of work waiting for me at home!

DAY 69, JUNE 8 - WEST FALMOUTH, LOOKING IN

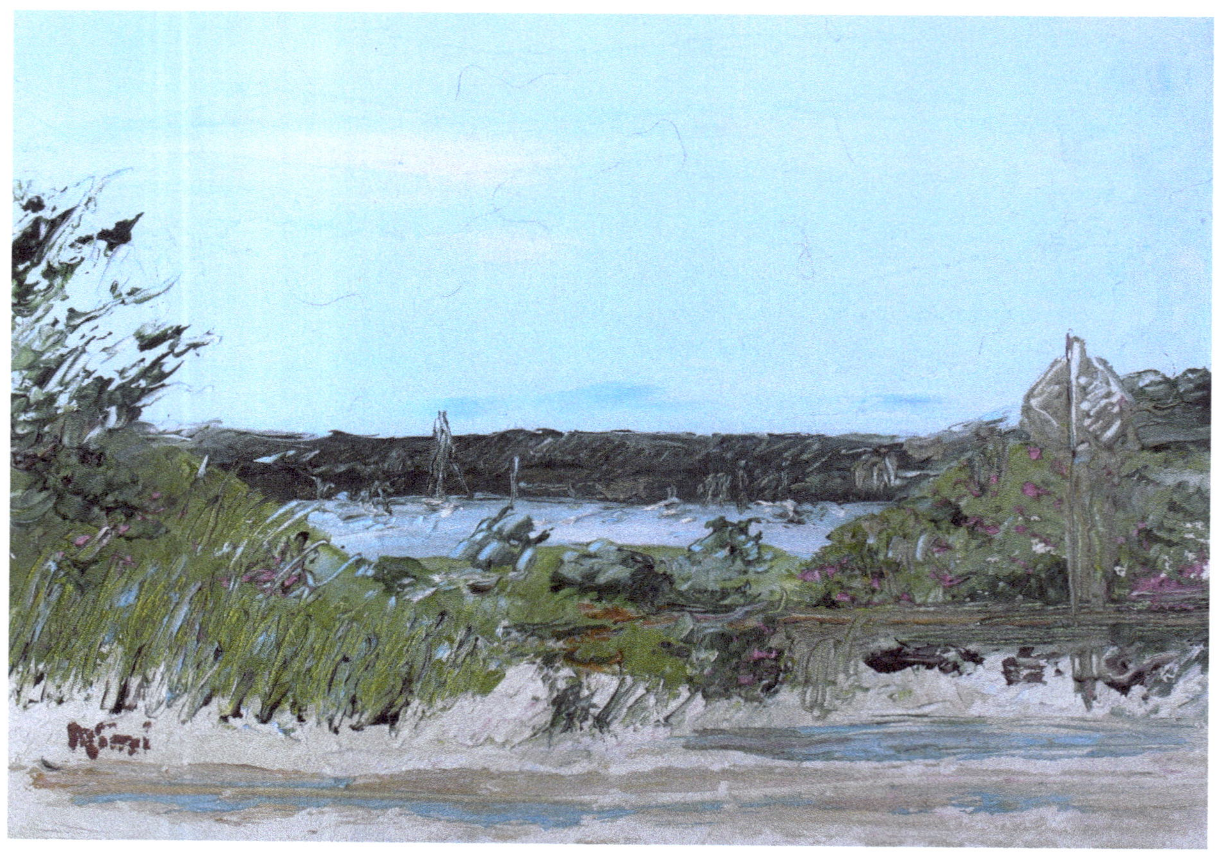

Painted early morning. When one leaves the Chapoquoit Beach parking lot, this is the view into West Falmouth Harbor inner harbor. So I suppose I could call it "same parking lot different view." Wanted to be sure to capture the rosa rugosa in bloom. This might be a fun idea for a larger painting.

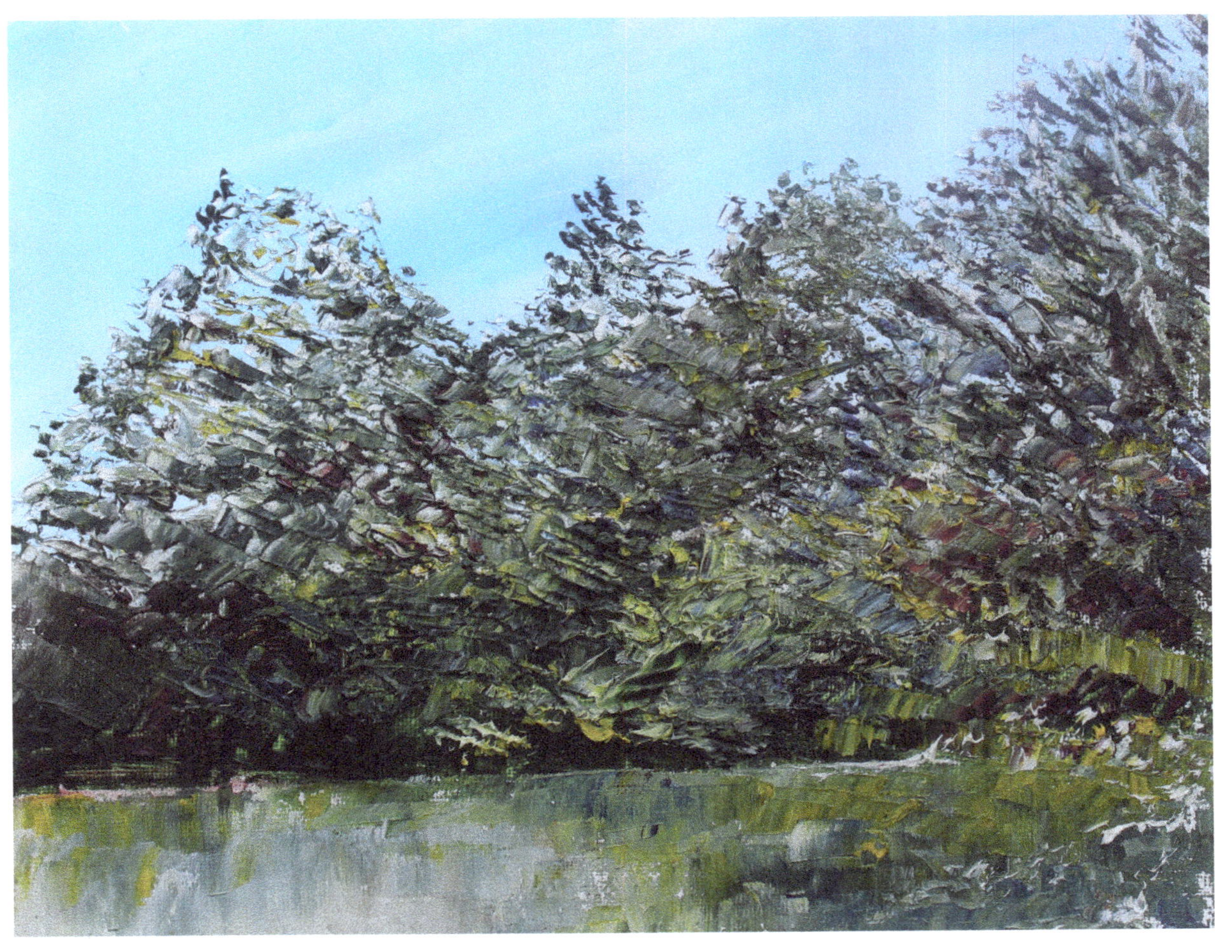

Painted in my backyard this evening because the trees are so lush and beautiful. Went impressionistic playing with color.

DAY 71, JUNE 10 - CHAPOQUOIT BEACH

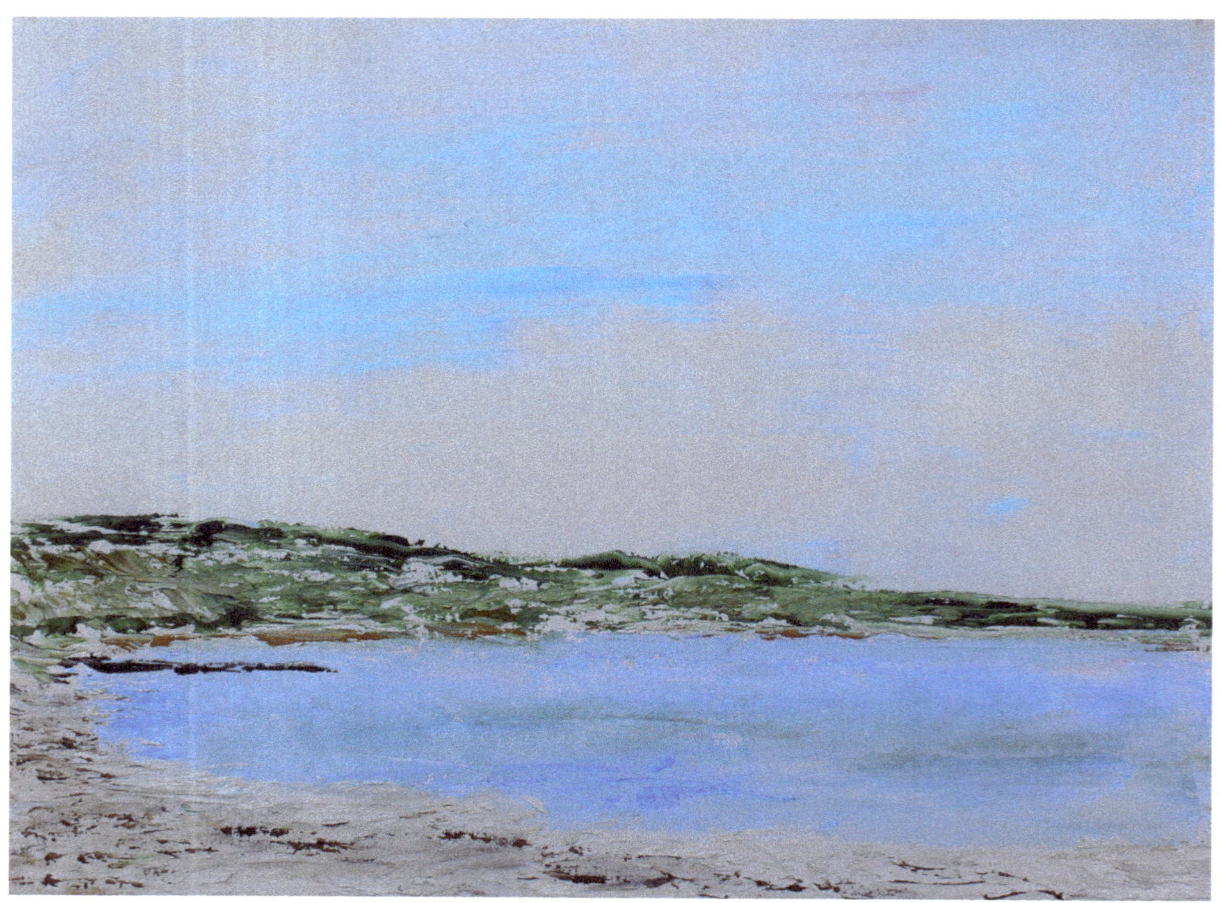

If you need some peace today...

DAY 72, JUNE 11 - CHAPOQUOIT BEACH

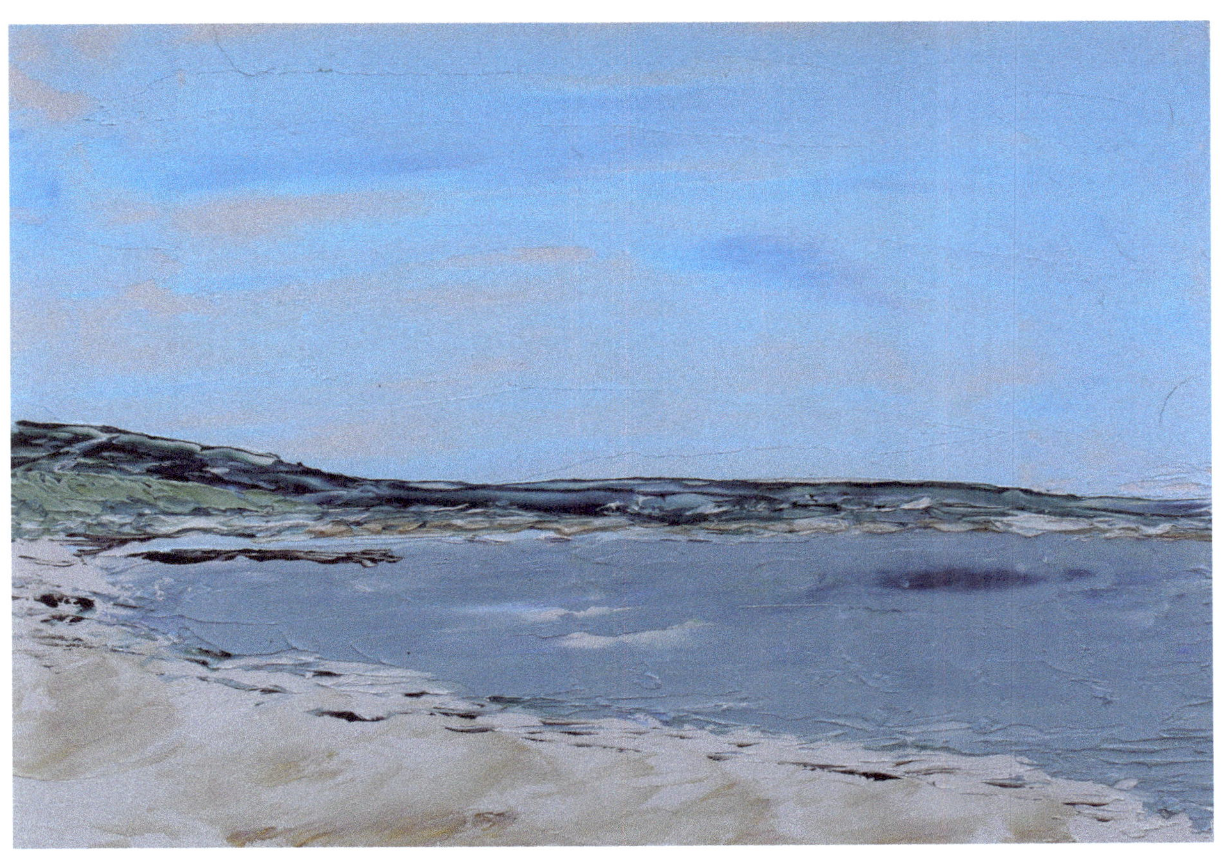

Happy weekend!

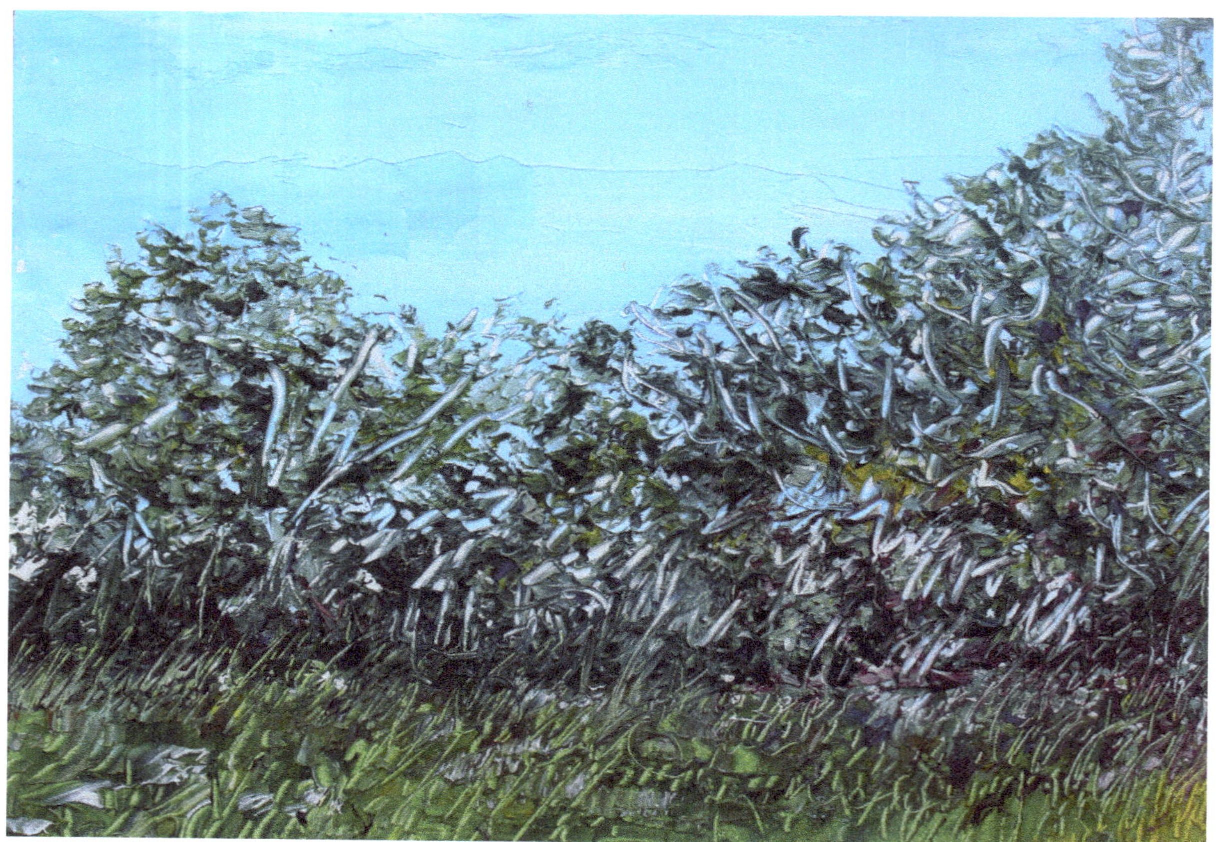

This is what happens when you realize it's 8pm and the natural light is almost gone and you haven't done your painting for the day yet and so think about ending the march to 100 days at 72 days because it was a self imposed goal anyway so what does it really matter except REALLY at 72 why would I not keep going to 100 but dinner is in the oven and smells soooo good.... soooooo back into the backyard I went and this little painting happened. Kinda Van Gogh-ish. Laid in some paint... then used the tip of the palette knife to scratch through it to bring out the light behind. whew!

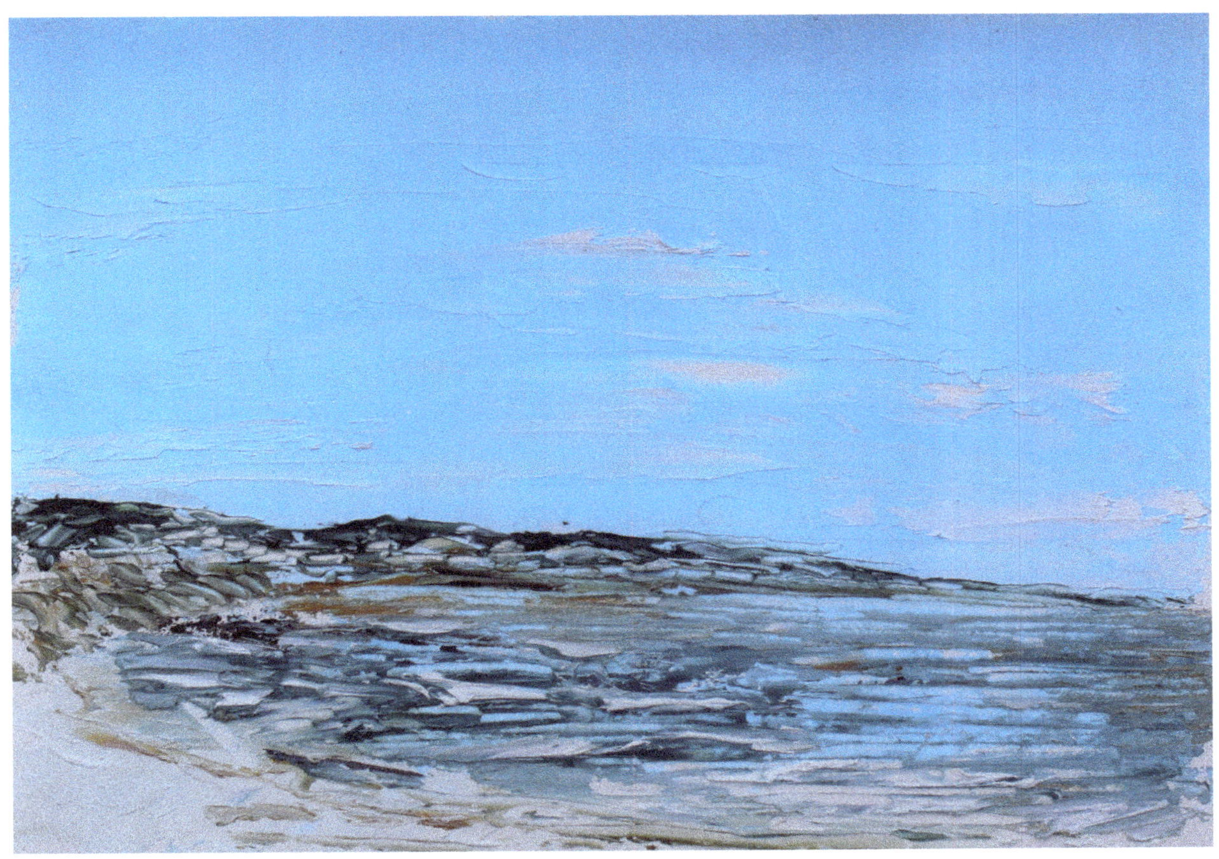

While I was there, a wedding happened on the beach! What a glorious place where we live!

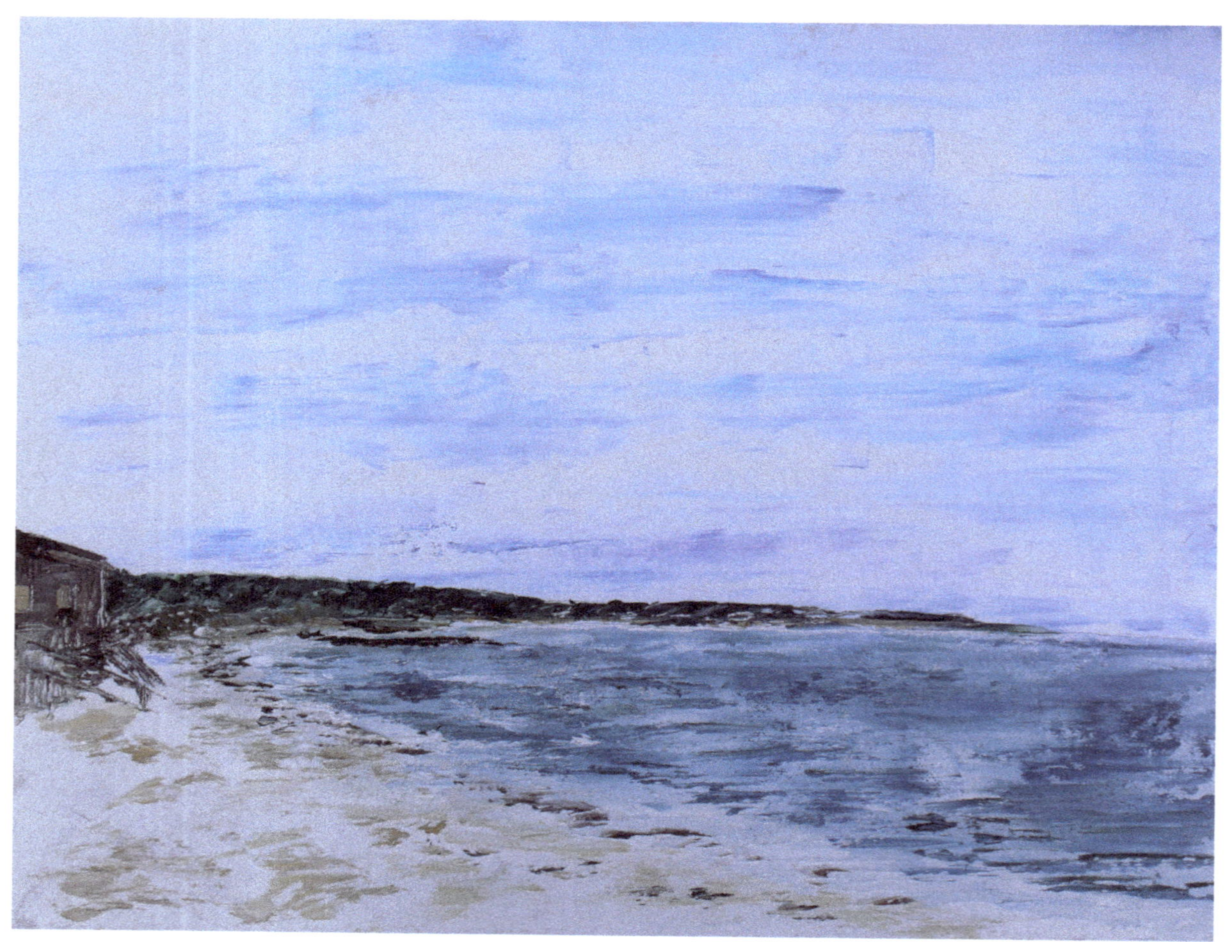

Yes. Chapoquoit again.

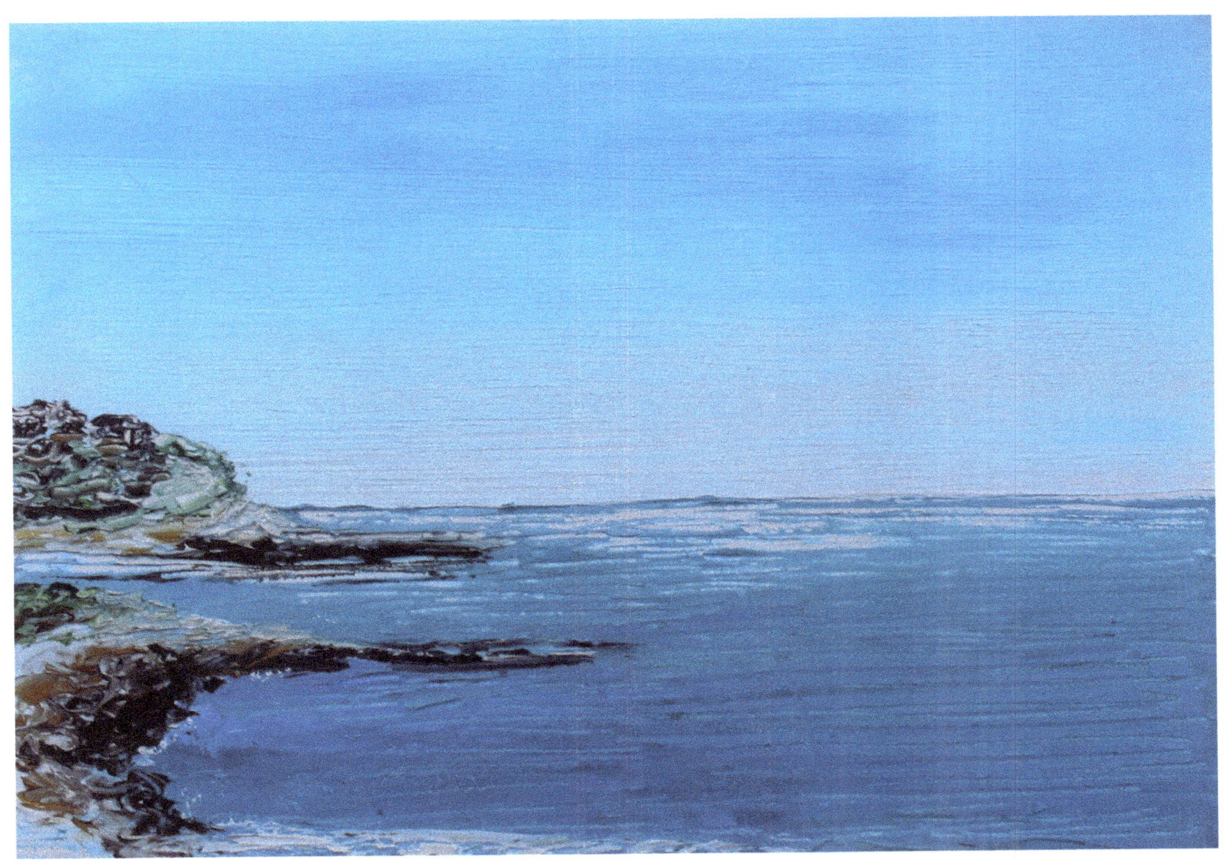

Looking across the mouth of Falmouth Harbor to the Heights, from Surf Drive Beach. I love the graceful curve of the road up the hill. I want to come back and do this one in pen and ink, with light watercolor wash.

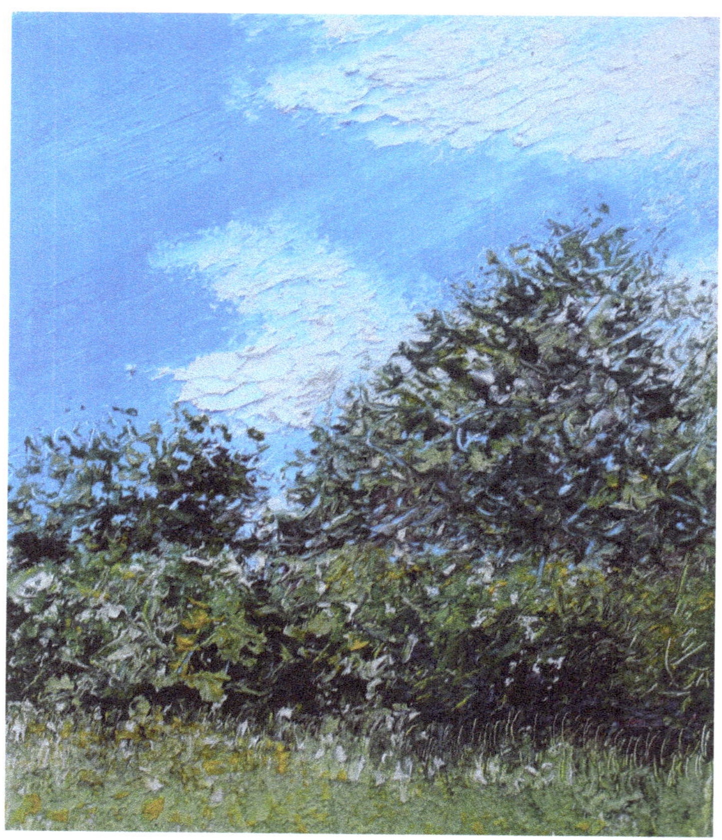

Painted in the backyard again this afternoon.

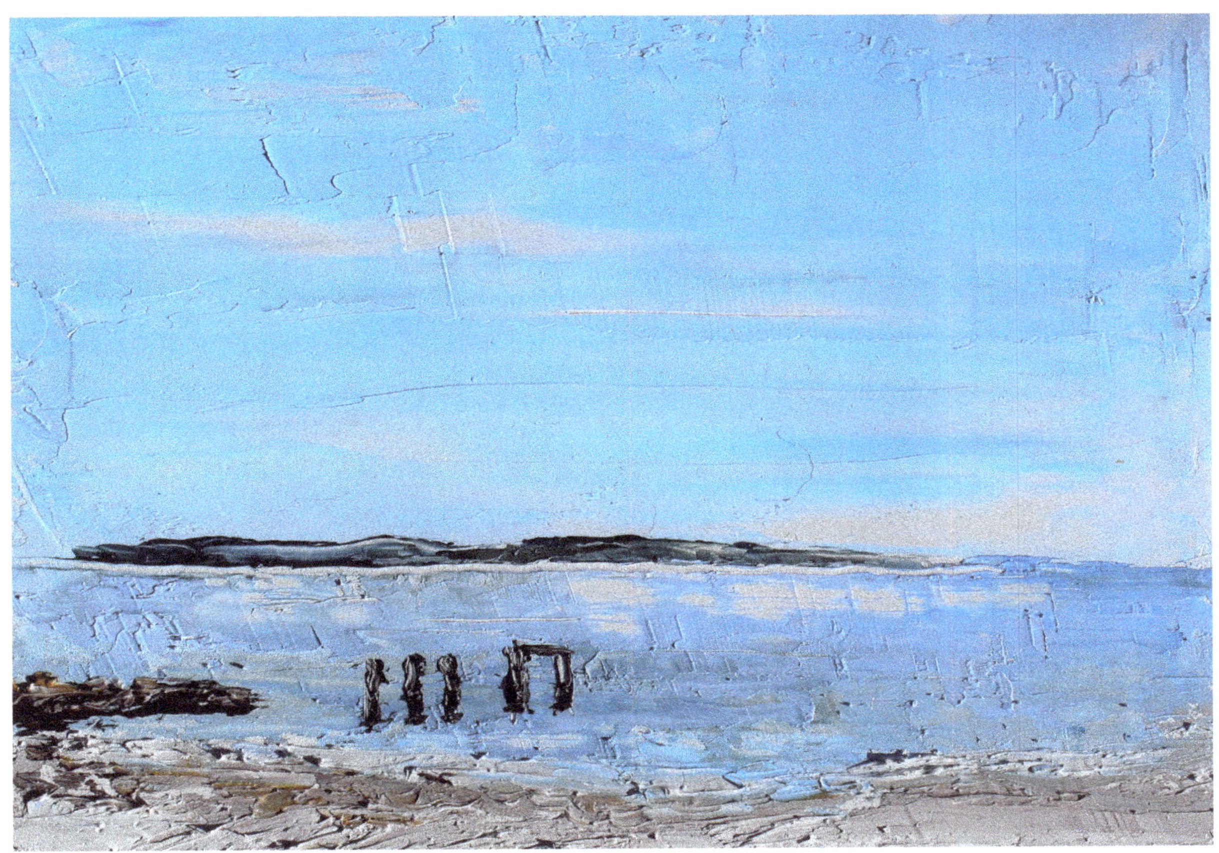

As I sat down to paint, a friendly couple asked me "are you Mimi?" "Why, yes, I am," I answered. "how do you know me?" "We follow you on Facebook," they replied. Feeling the Fabulous Falmouth love. Thank you everyone! Challenged to get the sky to look smooth, as some sand from the beach unintentionally got mixed into the paint!

DAY 79, JUNE 18 - BACKYARD

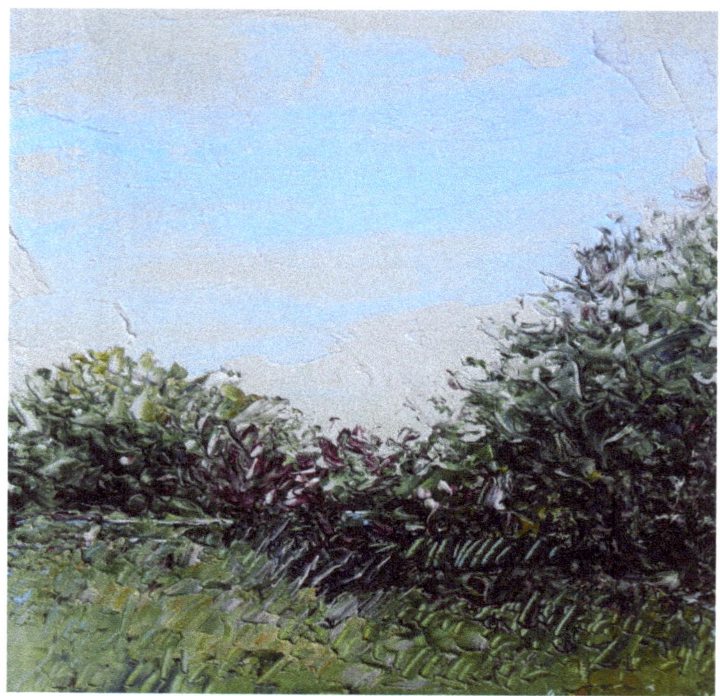

Another from my backyard, because it's fun!

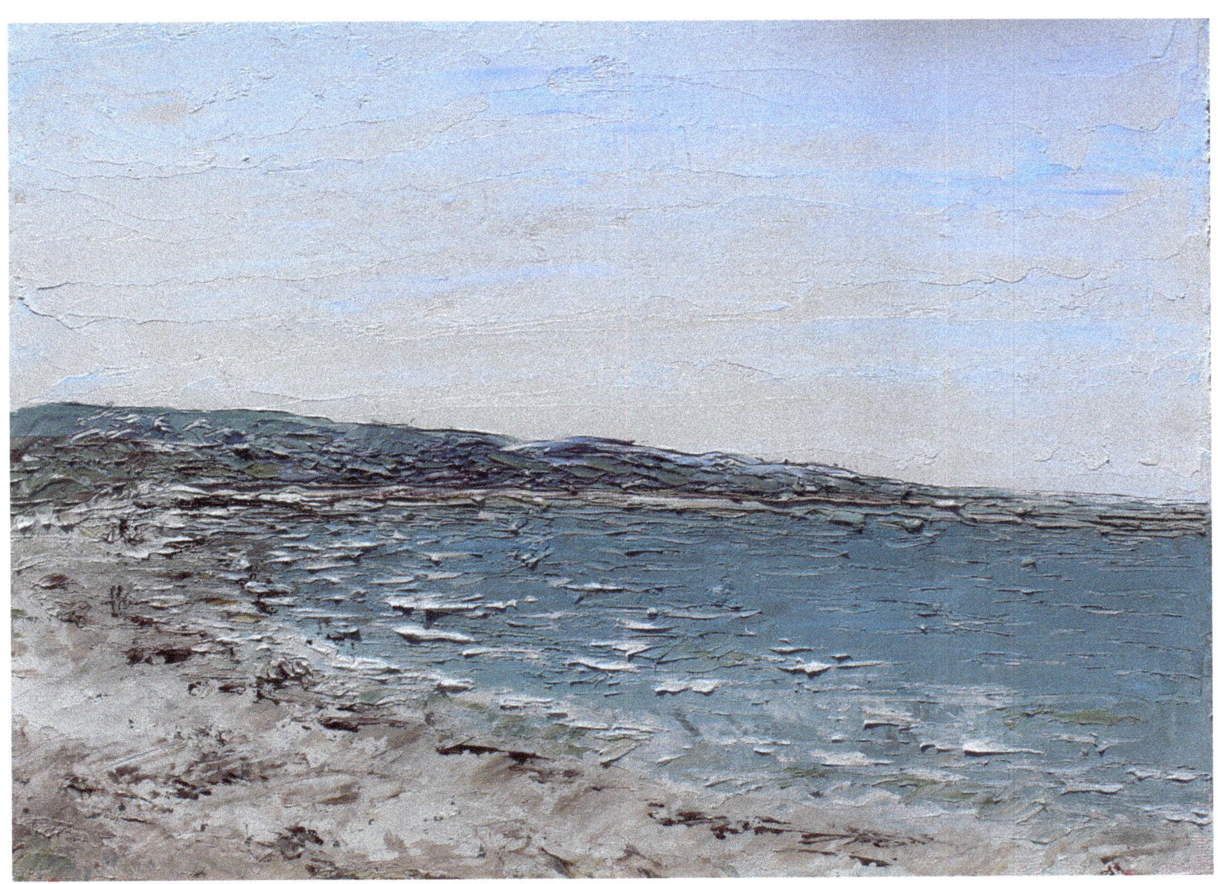

Wind and waves, and the painting knife kinda had a mind of its own! Happy Saturday everyone! How blessed are we to live in this most beautiful spot in God's creation?!

DAY 81, JUNE 20 - CHAPOQUOIT BEACH

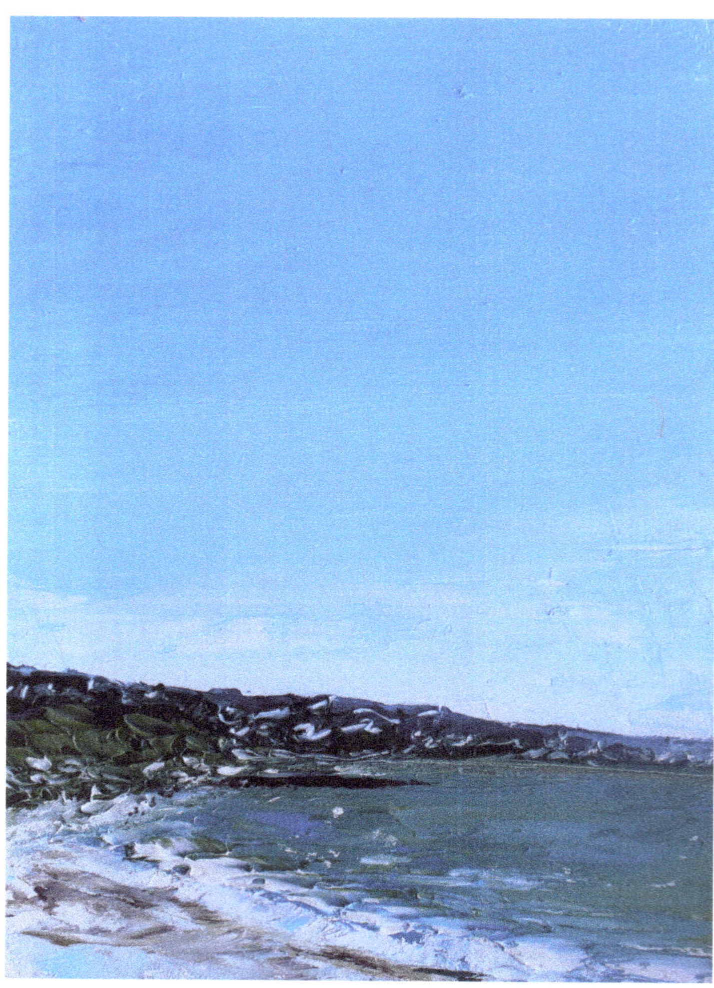

Heard a sermon today about changing our perspective in how we look at things,
so I thought it was a great time to flip the canvas 90 degrees.

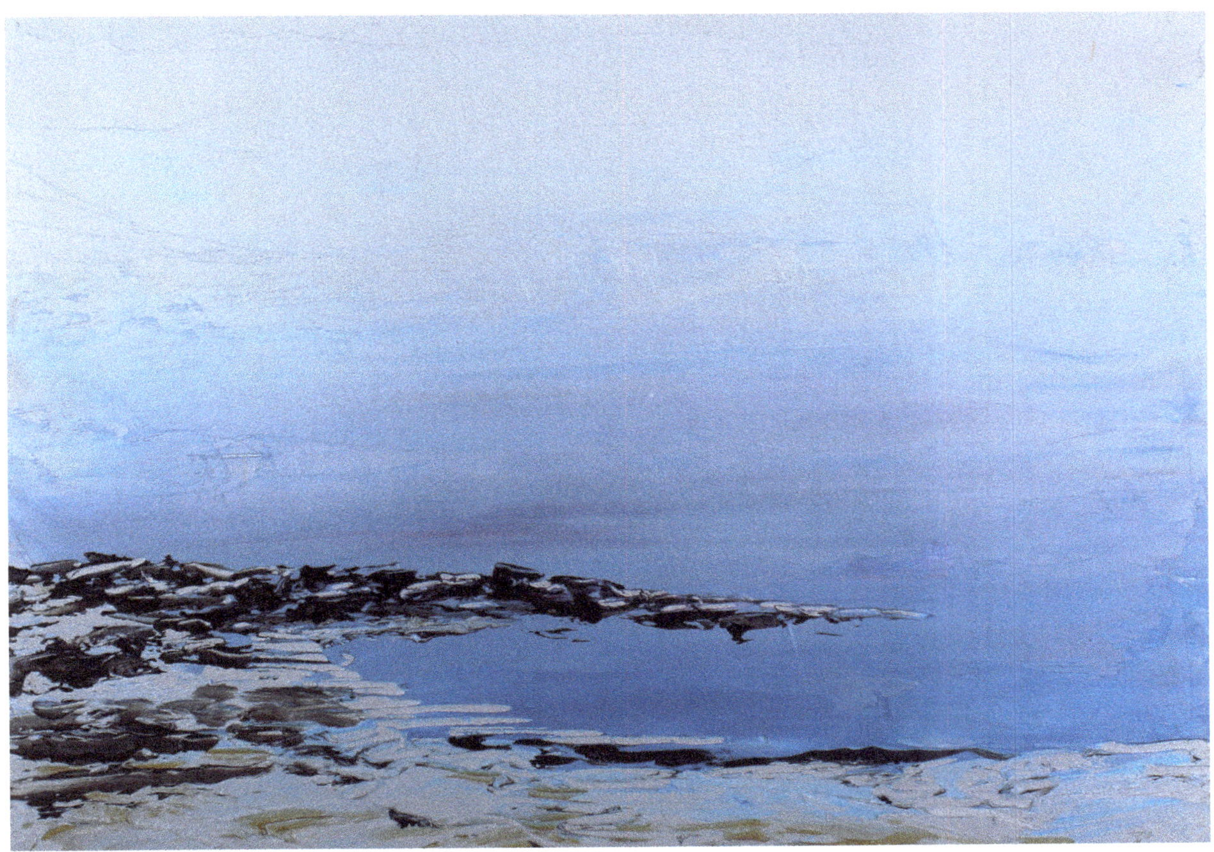

Foggy day painting. No horizon line. Edges blur, except for those up close. Surf Drive beach... but honestly it could be just about anywhere, couldn't it?

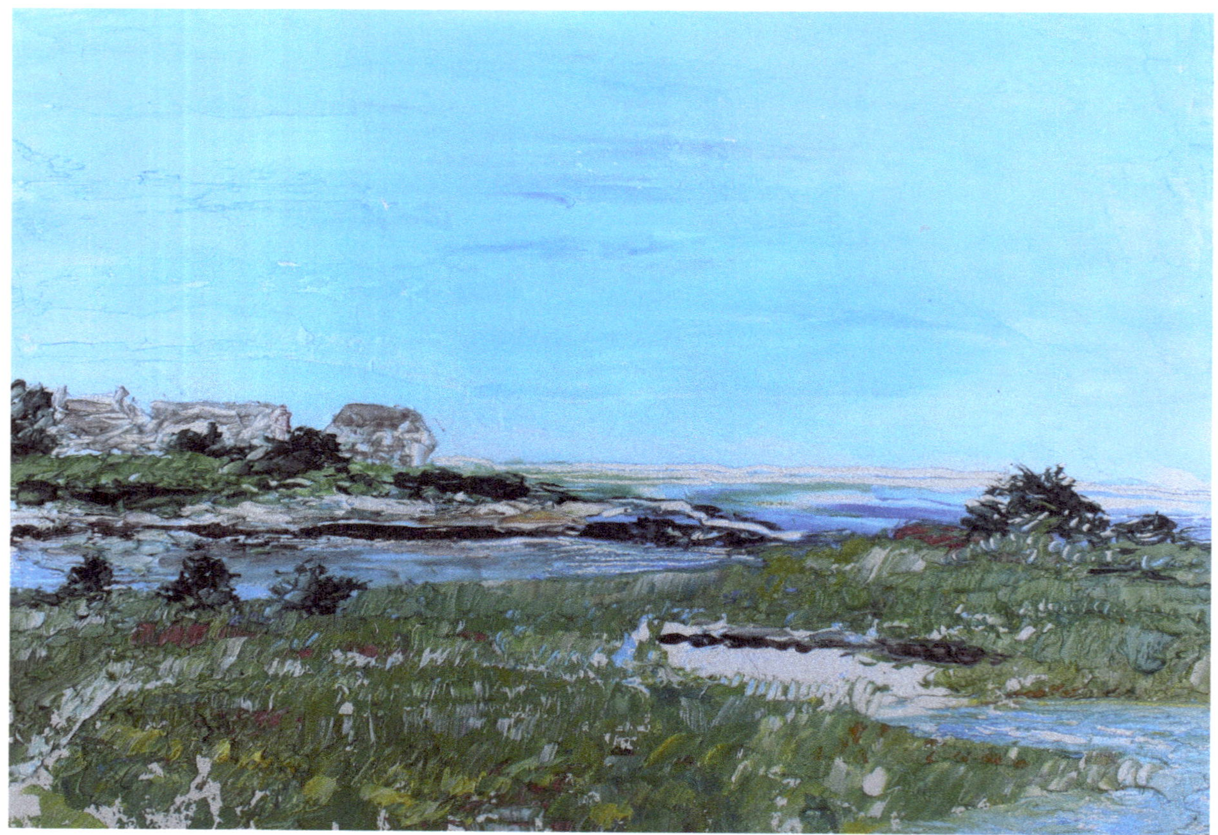

Parked at the end of the road to Little Island in West Falmouth. Peaceful, beautiful view. A place I've heard of more than I've been. A delight of a new find for me. Oh what a beautiful morning!

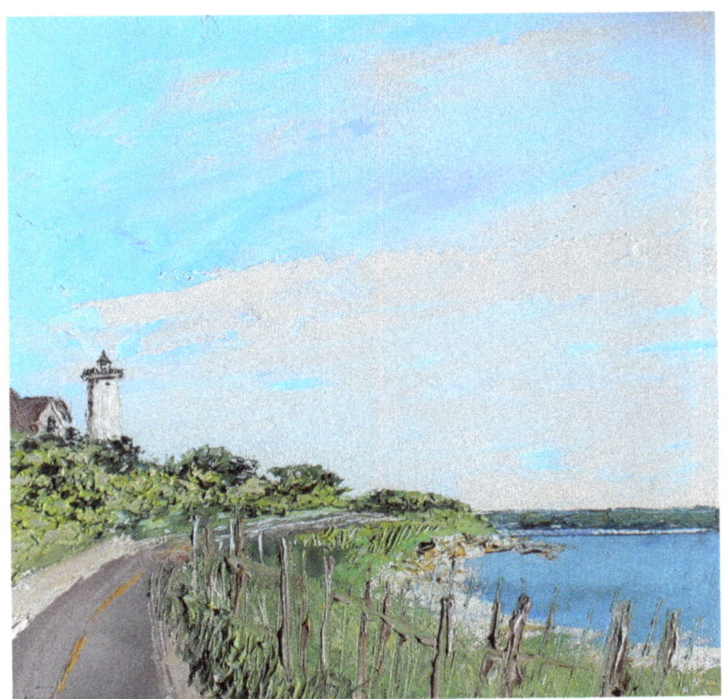

Nobska approach. SUCH a beautiful day to be on Cape Cod!

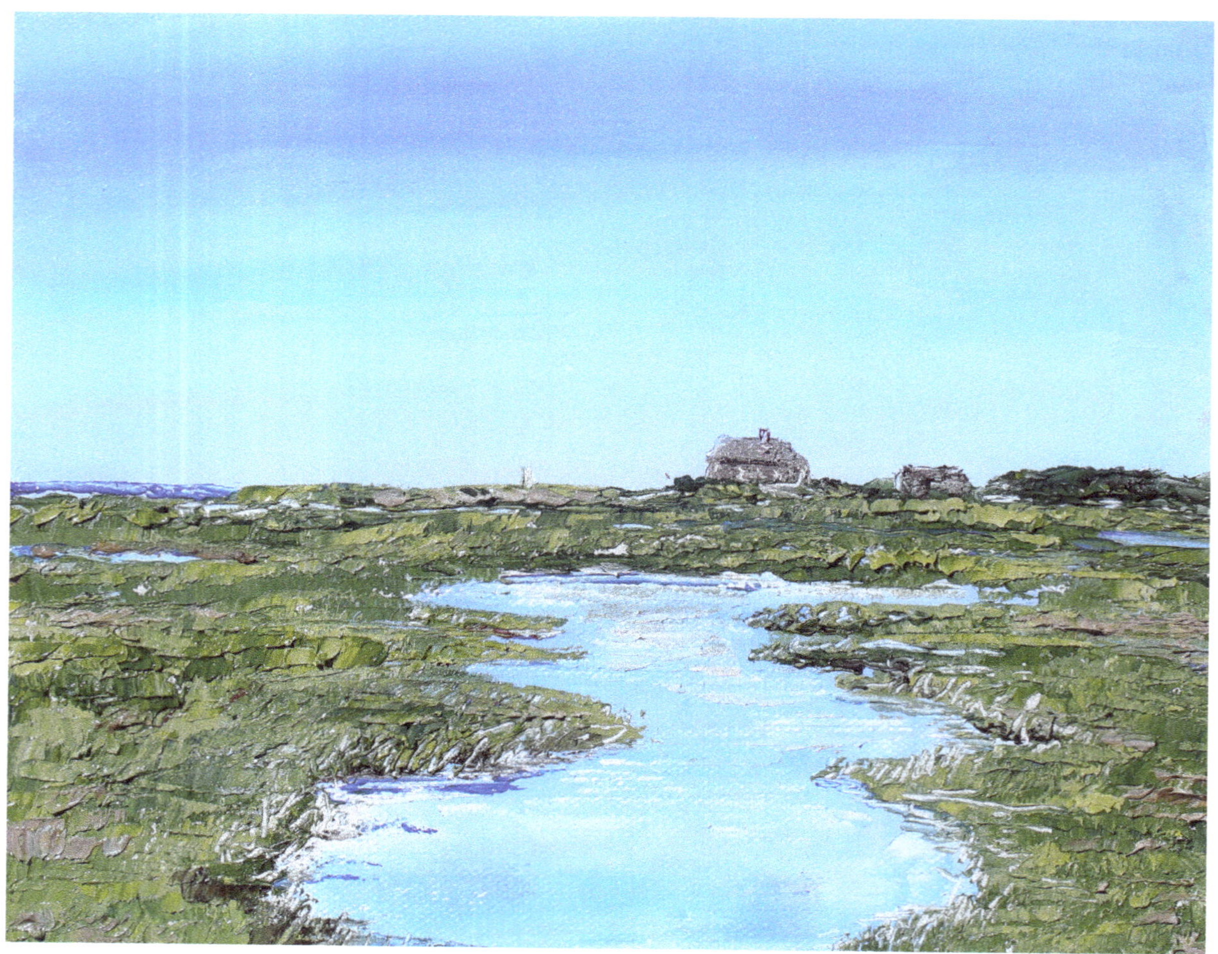

Great Sippewissett Marsh along the bike path. SO peaceful this morning. May paintI it again soon brushes rather than knife. The lush grass just begs to be tickled!

DAY 86, JUNE 25 - APPROACH TO CHAPOQUOIT ISLAND, WEST FALMOUTH

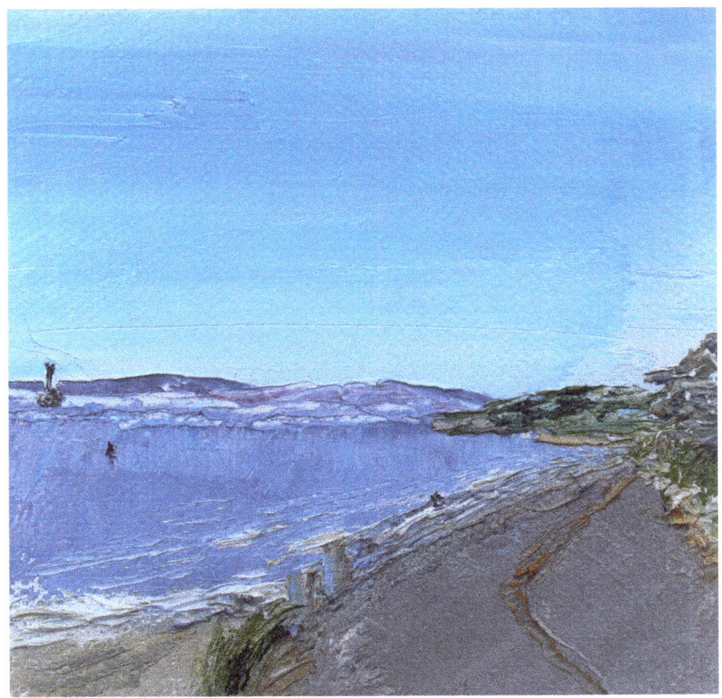

For those who say "I can't afford one of your paintings right now" I created the 'alla prima' line - paintings done on location in one sitting. Today's is extra budget friendly. A little 4"x4" stretched canvas oil painting of the approach road to Chapoquoit Island. Which is kinda funny and I suppose ironic given that the road leads to some of the 'higher budget' properties in West Falmouth!

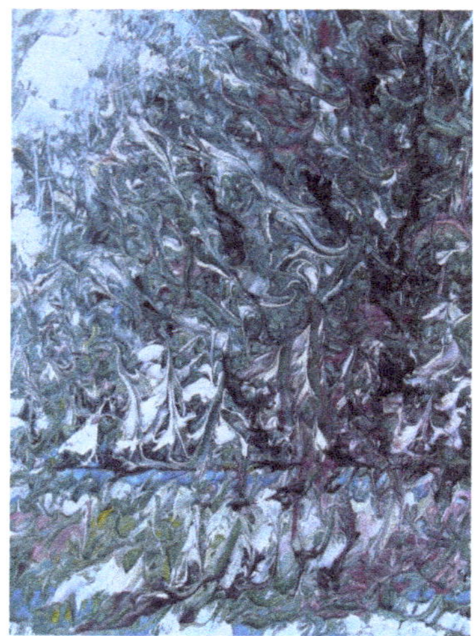

This began as a landscape in my
backyard then went off on its own as I
played with color and deep texture.
What adjective would you suggest?

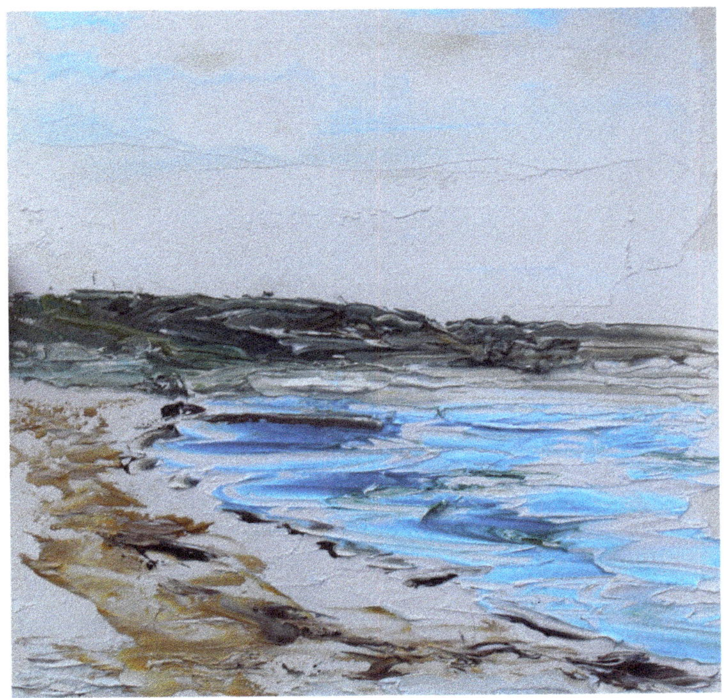

Chapoquoit Beach with wind and surf.

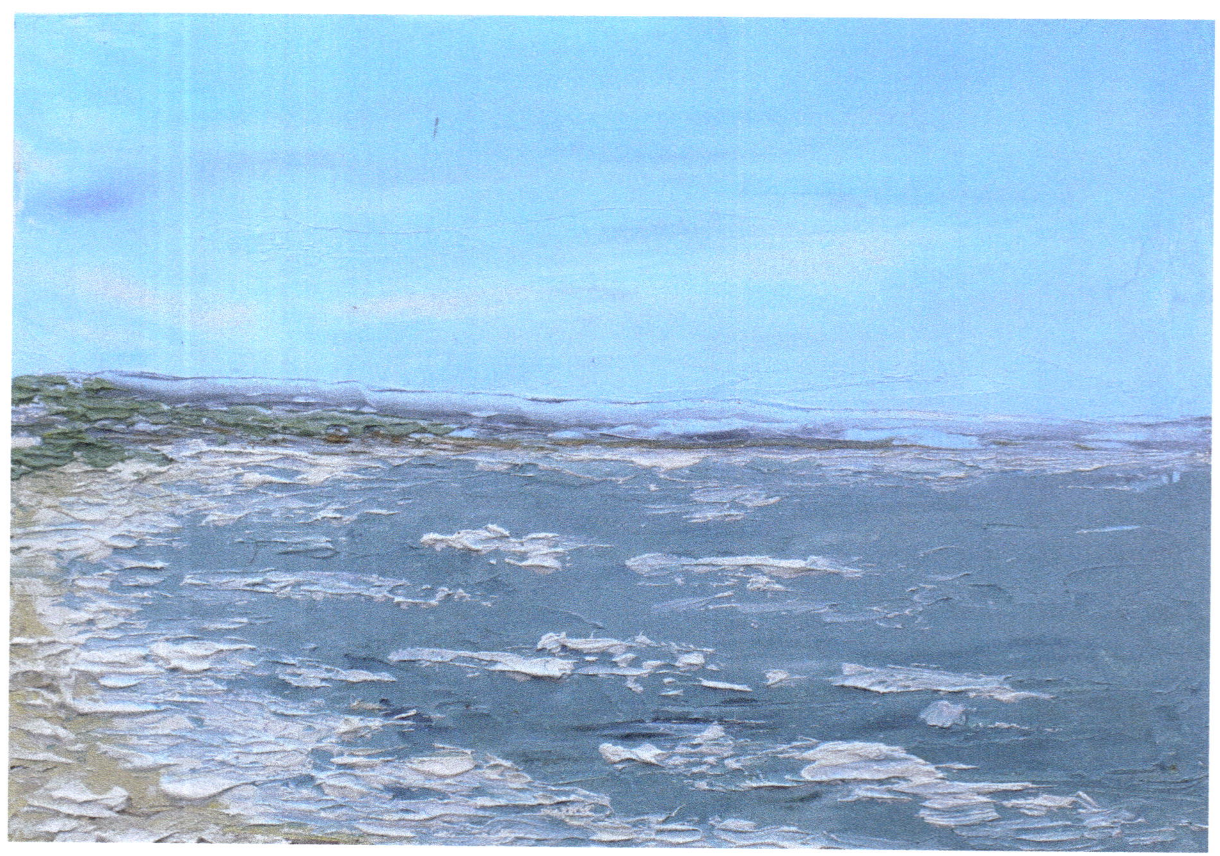

Grateful for the work I get to do.

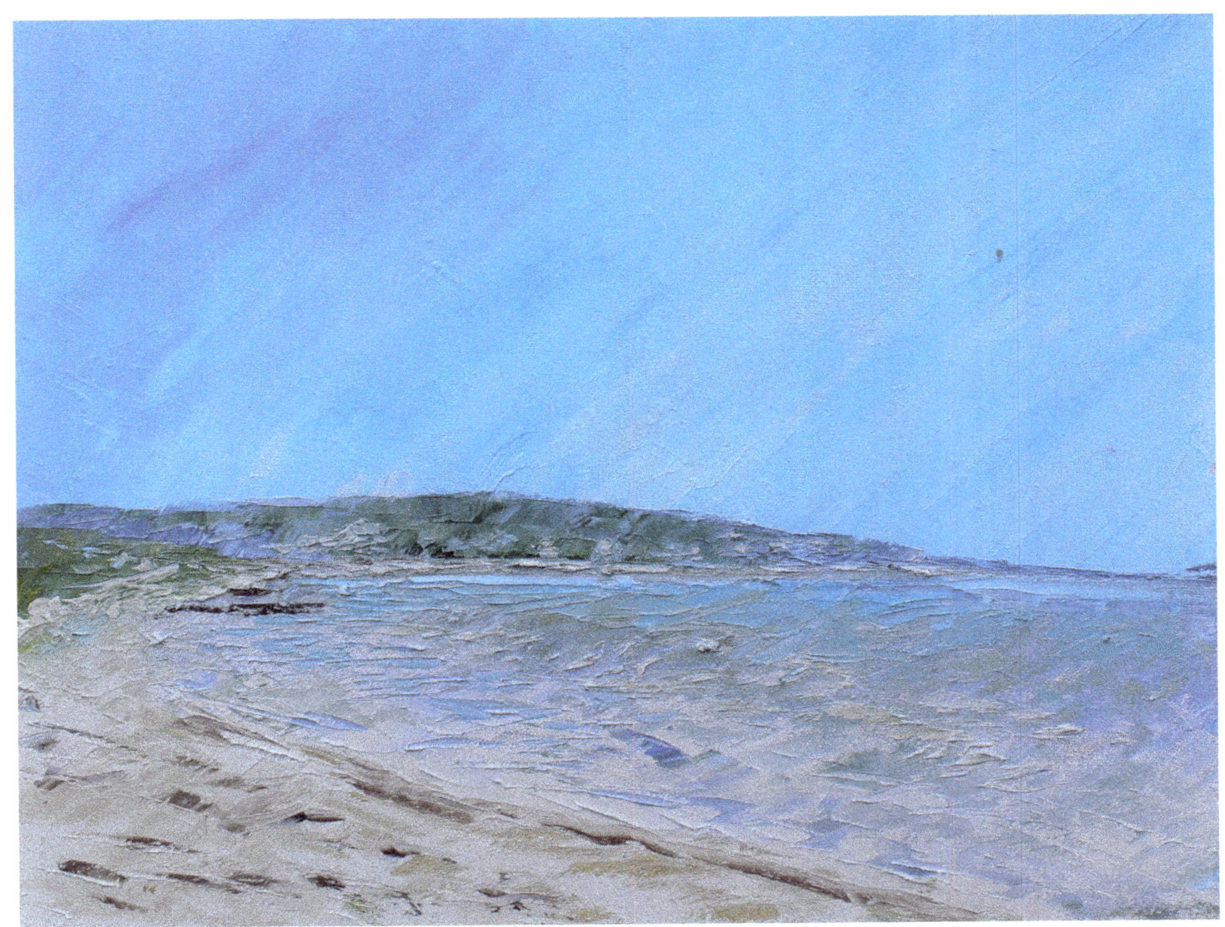

After sunset with a touch of fog.

DAY 91, JUNE 30 - SURF DRIVE BEACH

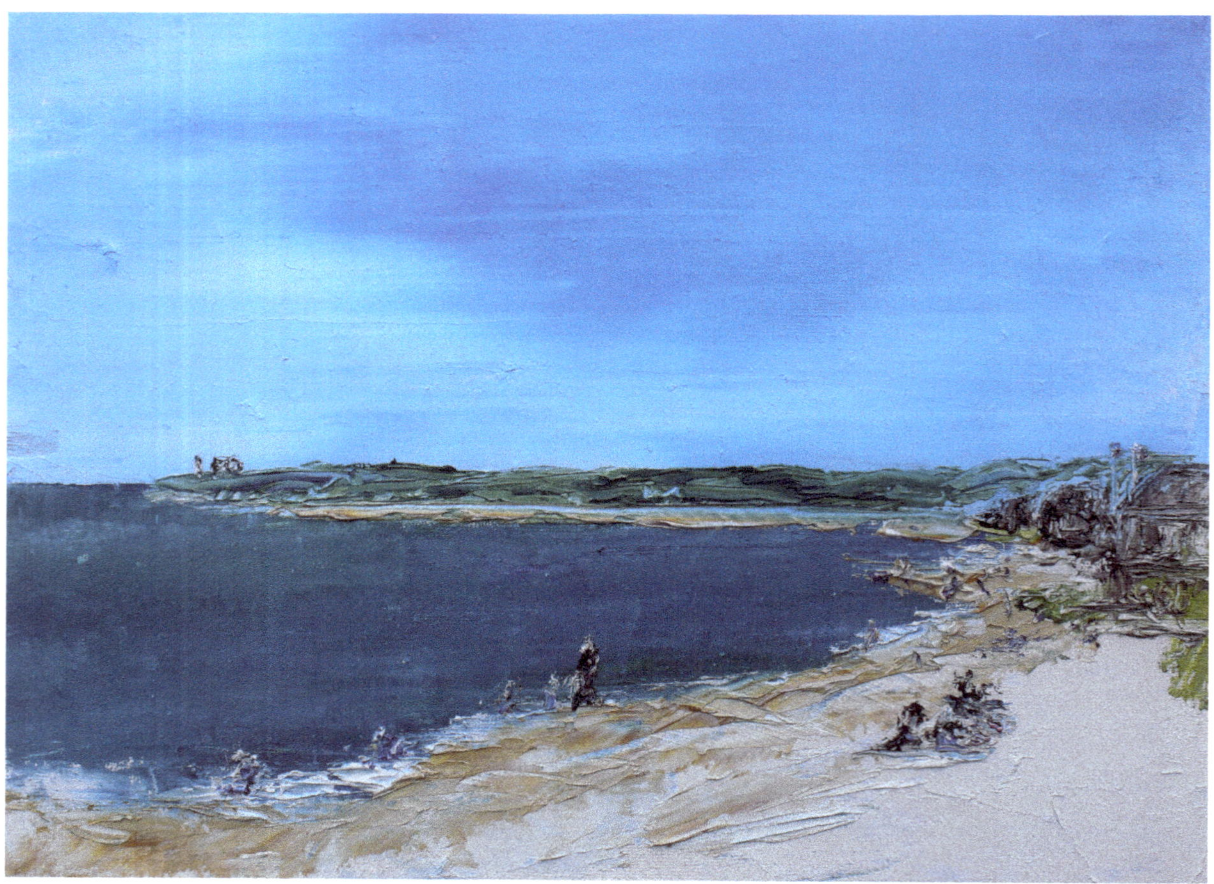

Out early this morning to Surf Drive Beach, a little further down the beach on the sand instead of from the parking lot.

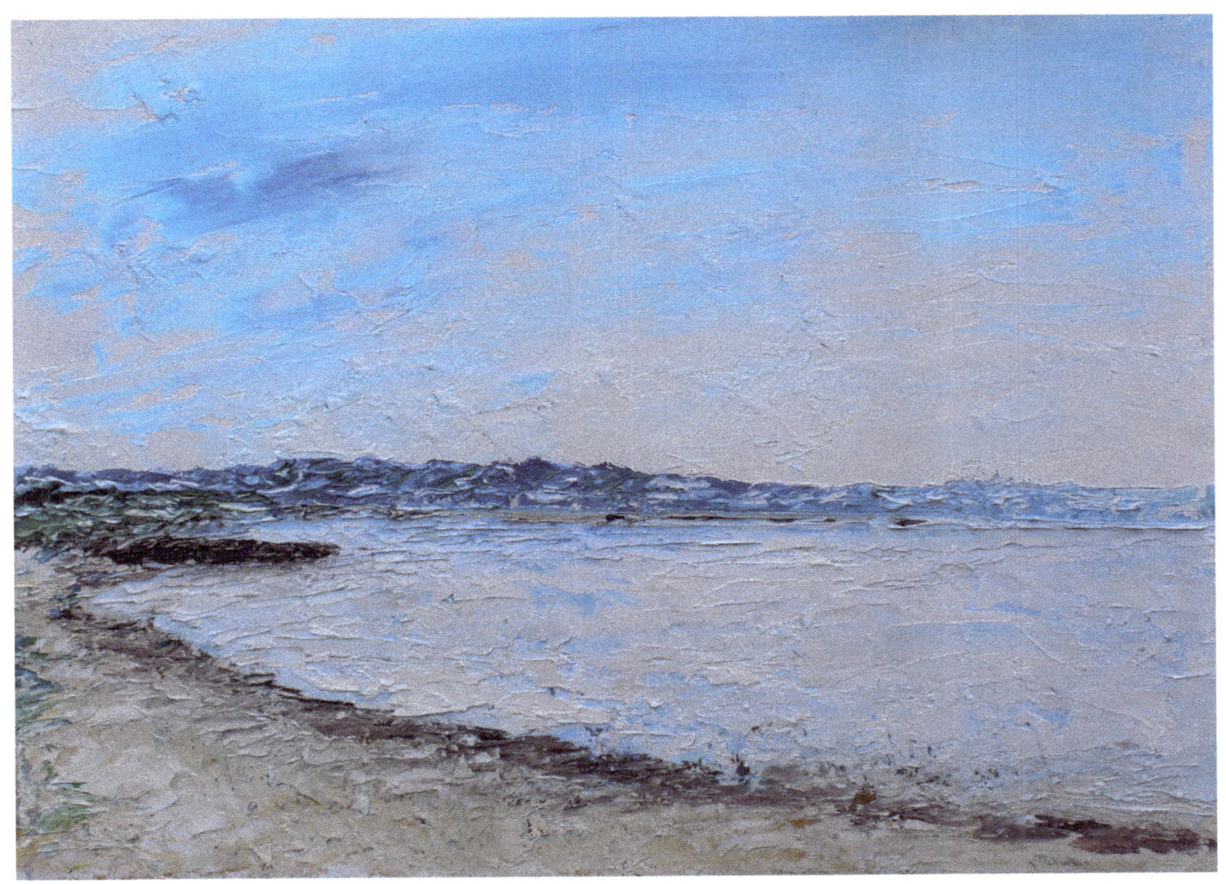

After the rain.

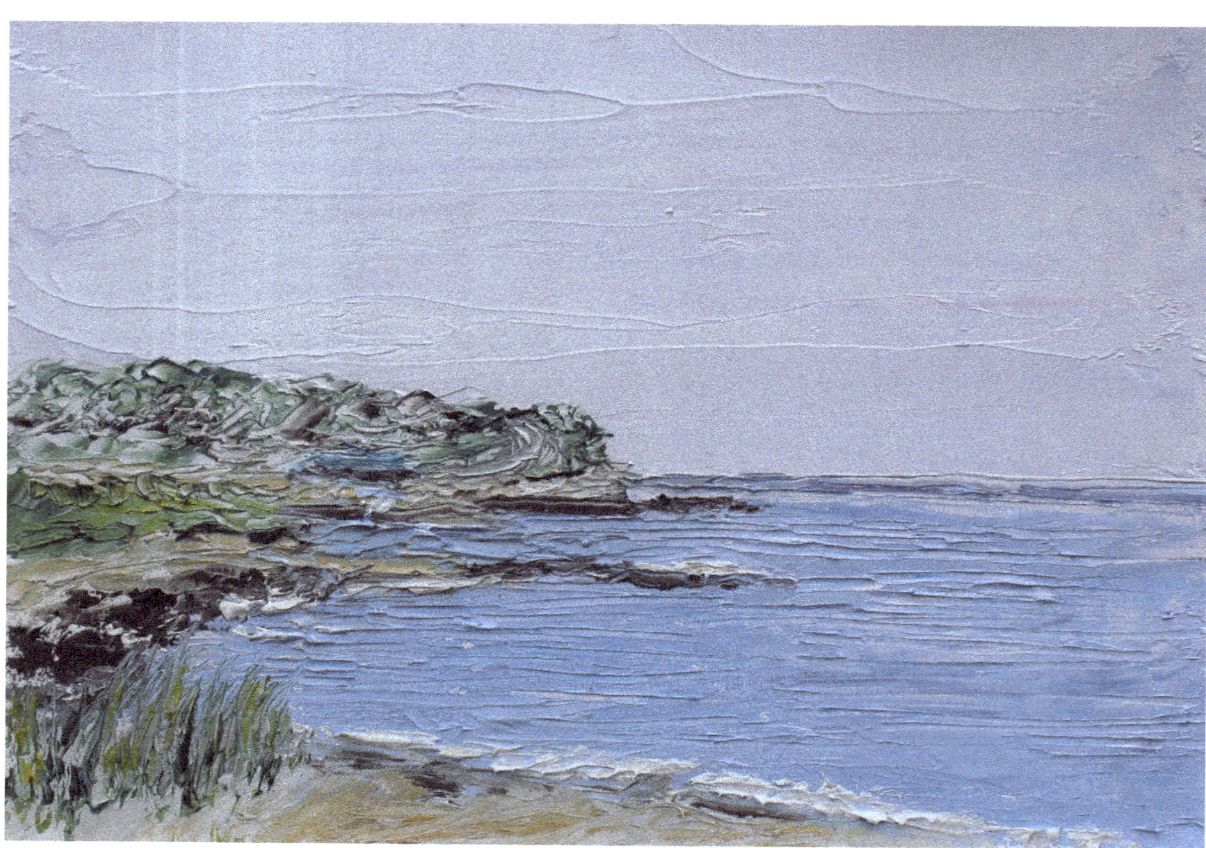

Yes, even on a grey and wet day, the atmosphere is delightful to paint. A spot I've grown fond of at the east end of the Surf Drive Beach parking lot, looking across the mouth of Falmouth Harbor to Falmouth Heights. I especially like the graceful curve of the road up to the top of the Heights, our own Falmouth Road Race version of heartbreak hill. Enjoy!

DAY 94, JULY 3 - SURF DRIVE BEACH SHACK

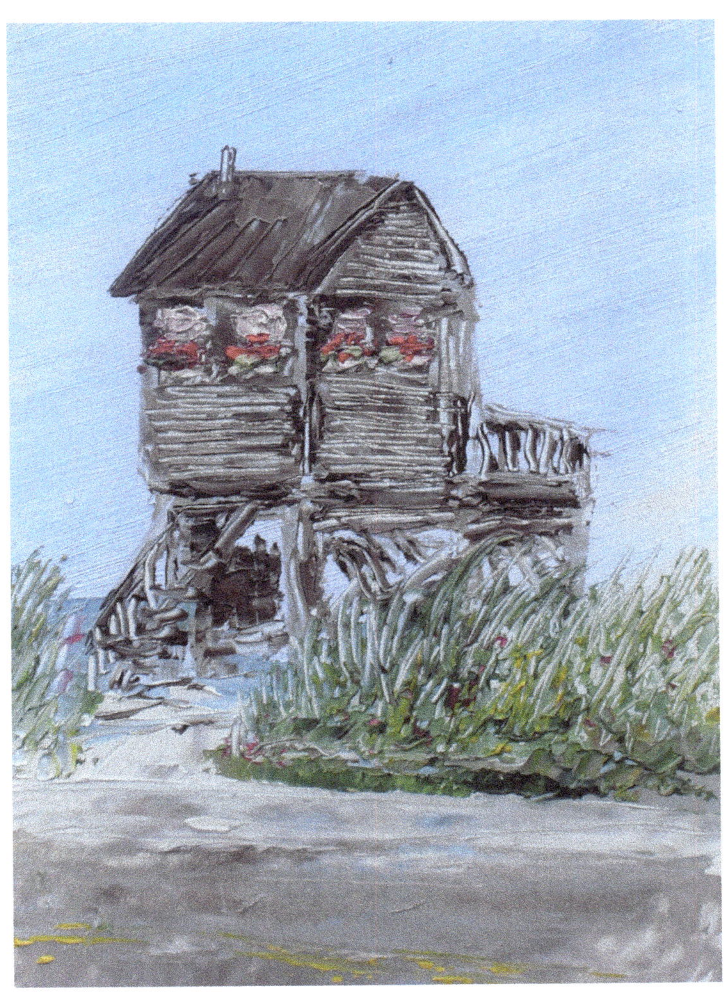

I've always wanted to paint the little houses on Surf Drive. It's a challenge to do architecture quickly and with painting knife wet into wet, but this was fun.

DAY 95, JULY 4 - FALMOUTH MAIN STREET

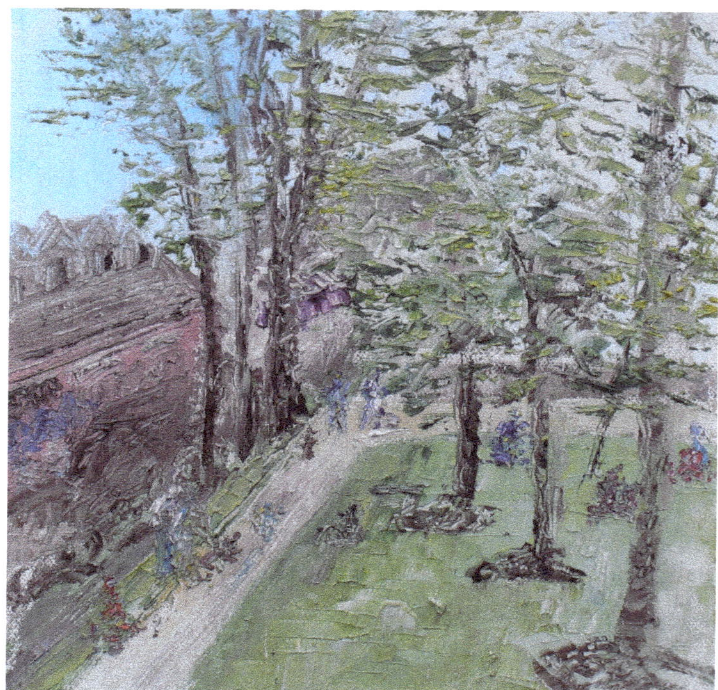

Main Street "How do you know when a painting is finished" is a question I hear often. Today the answer was - when the not in the forecast rain came down!!! Went into town to paint the folks at the College Light Opera Company July 4th concert, then learned it was cancelled, so sat at a table and painted anyway! Kinda silly Main Street scene. Challenging to paint so much detail quickly so this is truly 'impressionism'!!! Happy 4th everyone!

DAY 96, JULY 5 - CHAPOQUOIT BEACH

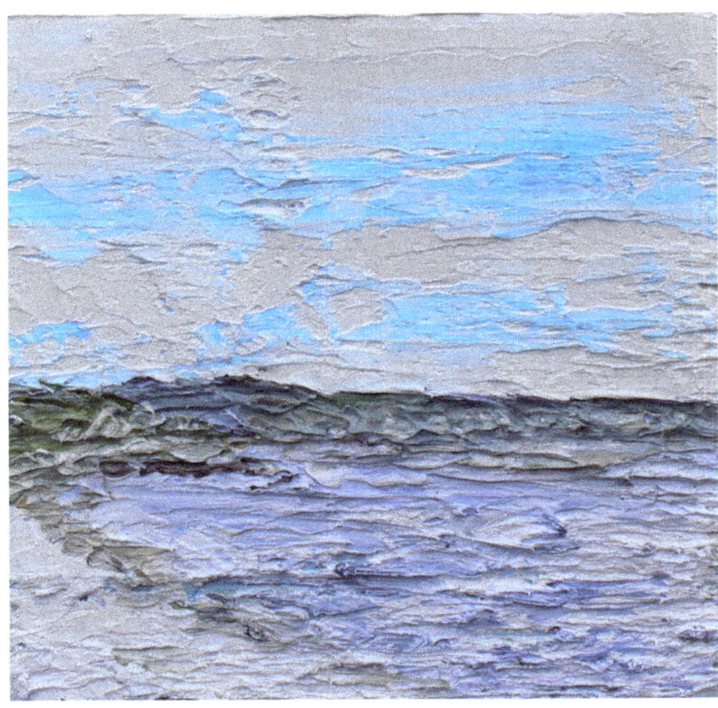

Grateful for sun, blue skies, and slightly warmer temps. How will you enjoy this beautiful day?

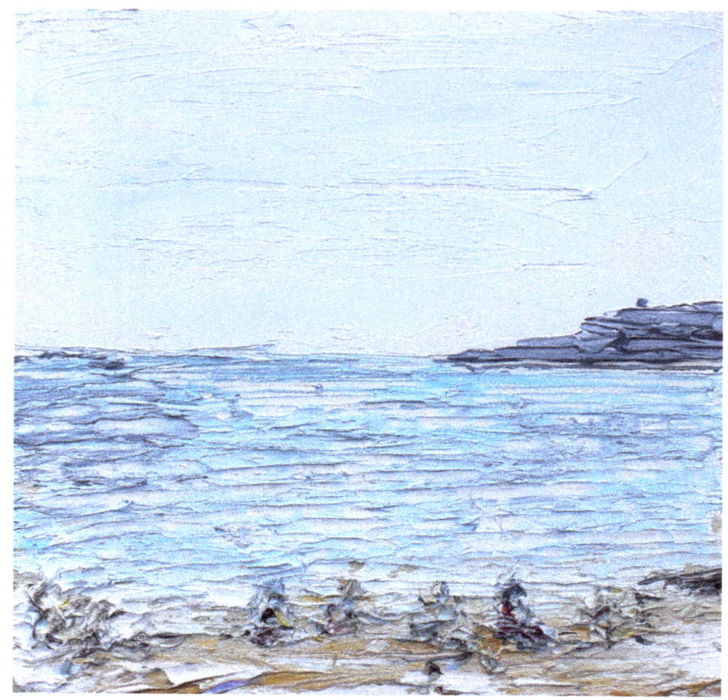

Fun to suggest some figures on the beach.

DAY 98, JULY 7 - GRASSLANDS

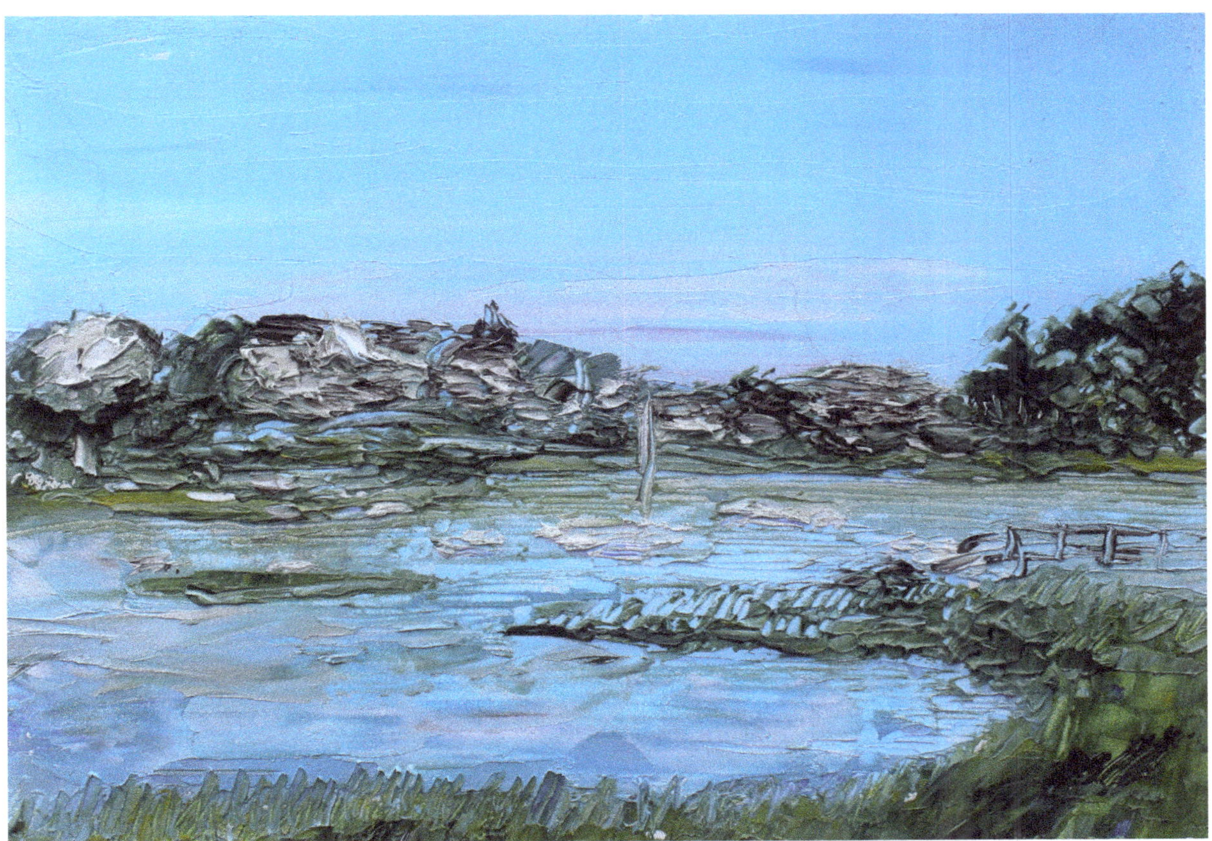

At the end of Grasslands Road in Cataumet, looking at the north side of Lawrence Island and into Squeteague Harbor. Vaguely. Working small with painting knife wet paint into wet paint, it is a challenge to capture as much detail as I would have liked.

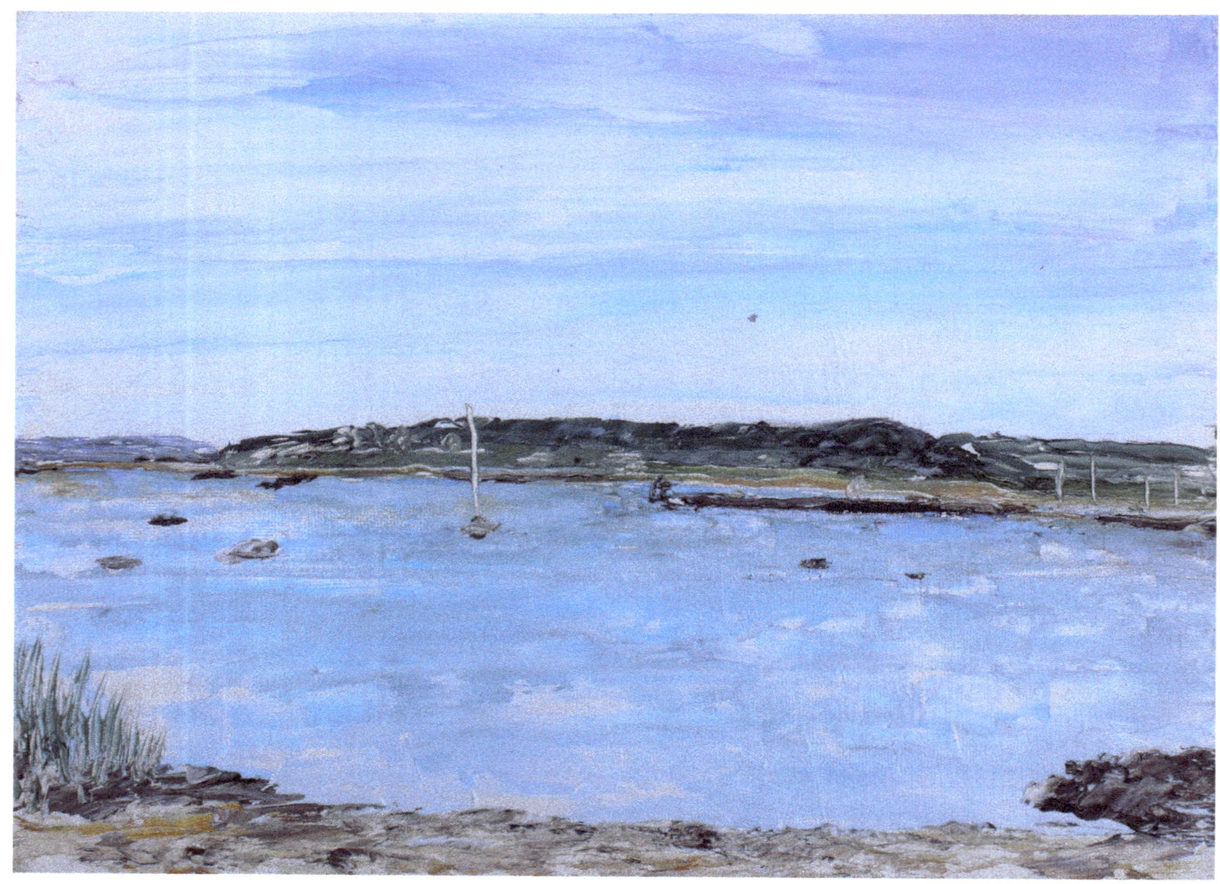

I was blessed by the kindness of someone who lives there to paint in my happy place today. A painted study in preparation for a larger commission painting of similar view, looking into Megansett from outer Megansett.

DAY 100, JULY 9 - CHAPOQUOIT BEACH AND BOWERMAN'S SWIM RAFT

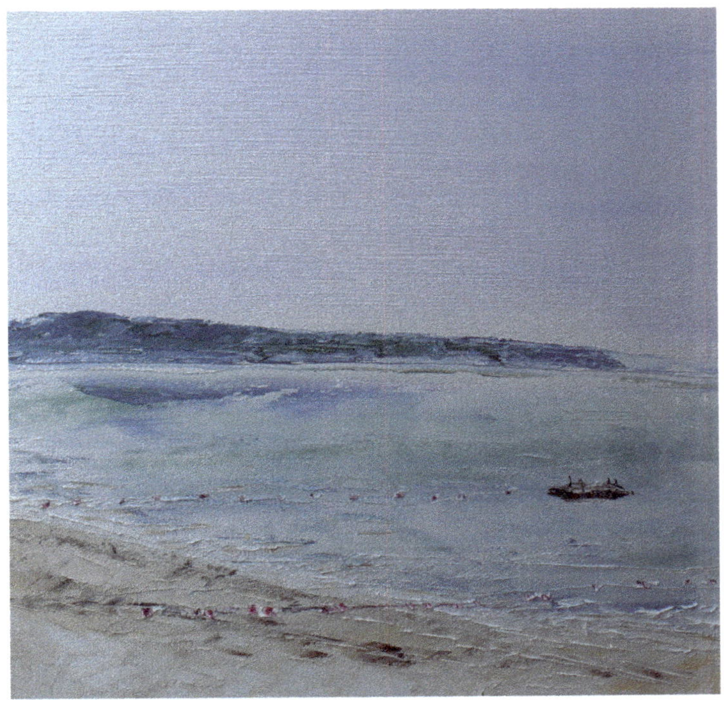

Even in the rain - got it done! Painting through the windshield wipers at Chapoquoit Beach. Fun colors. Included the swim dock and lines going out into the water from Bowerman's Beach Club.

THE FINALE

Ask *"what's your favorite Falmouth beach"* and you will likely get an immediate response, without a moment's pause.

Answers come from the heart. From precious memories. From childhood, or time shared with family and friends.

"My children loved to play there."

"My husband proposed to me there."

"I love the sunsets there."

Similar reasons with varied locations.

One of the personal joys of this project for me was in discovering, and rediscovering, beaches other than the two I most often frequent.

Megansett was my first Cape beach, back when I was 8 years old. I returned there often at different times of my life, with different significant friends, in different seasons. It's seen me through tears of joy, and the other kind.

Chapoquoit? I didn't know it existed until my mother moved here in 1988. It was the place where I first saw wind-surfers, on a cold January day. Their technology has improved through the years, but on a brisk windy day, oh yes, they are still there. Likely even some of the same people. It's also the beach closest to home for me now. It's my first and last swim of the season. My nap in the sun on a late September afternoon.

Old Silver? Not on my usual list. Another friend shared with me it is her favorite, together with her late husband. Cherished memories of their engagement there.

Stoney Beach, in Woods Hole? Locals claim it as their own. The town lists it as theirs. Does it really matter? Seems like every time I was there the wind and water were wild. Yet still beautiful.

Grew's Pond in Goodwill Park? Honestly, I only painted it twice. Though the town lists it on their website, it's not salt water, and that's what defines a beach, for me.

Woodneck is a favorite of families with young children, with a non surf-side area where they can safely play. It was also the one where I had to leave the front seat of my car to paint on the beach, since there is no view of the water from the parking lot.

Surf Drive Beach? Years ago I did a lot of writing, and it was my 'go to' place. Perhaps because I rarely saw anyone there I knew, so there were less distractions. And it's fun to watch the ferries come and go to Martha's Vineyard. I also discovered a cool view across the mouth of Falmouth Harbor to Falmouth Heights from the east side of the parking lot

 Bristol Beach, and Falmouth Heights They're like close cousins, right down the road from one another. The Heights, holding memories of many 4th of July evenings watching the spectacular Falmouth fireworks. And Bristol Beach, unknown to me until a man friend introduced me to it several years ago.

That leaves one. Menauhant. While it is not the one where I go to to swim, or sit in the sun, or read, or nap, it is perhaps the single most sacred, to me, and many others. My nickname for it is 'Baptism Beach,' because it was there, on September 20, 2015, I went down into the waters and came back up again refreshed and renewed, proclaiming in public my faith in Jesus Christ. That's an experience that marks a place as sacred.

Or in the words of Pastor Ben Feldott of Cape Cod Church, *"Menauhant Beach is sacred sand...that sounds surprising to some...it's on the wrong side of Falmouth...the sand is finer on the other side. But for the hundreds who have walked with me down into those waters for one of the church's annual baptism services...you know just what I mean."*

THE THANK-YOU'S

Writing thank you's at the end of a book is a dangerous thing, as it is far too easy to omit someone obvious. To whomever I might have left out - please accept my apology.

I will begin with a huge THANK YOU to the members of the "Fabulous Falmouth" Facebook group, who have offered encouragement, support, comments, likes, loves, and wows in response to my postings. You turned my project into something much more significant than I originally envisioned when several of you shared that you looked forward to the daily postings, and found them bringing you peace in the midst of the hectic. THANK YOU.

The life of an artist, or at least this artist, means spending a ton of time alone, and in the past 12 months, even more so. To read such lovely comments and words of appreciation - well, you warm my heart. Bring smiles to my face. And give me the extra 'that a girl' nudges that keep me painting and posting.

Thank you to each of you who purchased a painting during the 54 days, many of you as generous gifts for others.

Thank you to the employees and board members of the Town of Falmouth, and to all who work to keep our beaches the beautiful places they are.

Thank you to Edmund Beard, always at the ready when I call and say, *"hey, I have some new writing for you to proofread."* His eagle eye and quick turnaround time are a writer's dream.

Thank you to my new friend and fellow artist book author Heidi, whose professional knowledge of graphic design was so generously offered and appreciated as I prepared this new edition.

Thank you to Pastor Ben Feldott of Cape Cod Church for his quote in the finale about Menauhant Beach, and for his consistently on point preaching. I have learned SO MUCH in the past seven years from you and your staff. Life changing in the most wonderful ways.

Thank you Betsy, Jane, Jill, Leiko, Meredith, Susan, and Tammy for your prayer support as I create. I had to place your names in alphabetical order as you are all equally important! As are a whole bunch of others of you unnamed here.

To Susan, and her character known as the Magic Crayon, another creative using her gifts to inspire others.

To Laura, for nearly 25 years of being there to listen when I say *"here's my next idea!"*

Not sure I can adequately thank my daughter Anna - my social media guru and oh so wise advisor on so many things. It's a lovely thing when our children surpass us on the wisdom scale.

And last but by no means least, I thank God for the life path and inspiration to create "The 54" and for each and every friend who supports, encourages, and shares with me in this journey.

WHAT'S NEXT?

I am often asked "do you teach art lessons?" and I usually answer "no, not right now. I don't have a space to do it."

The more honest answer behind my answer is, "I no longer teach in person art classes because I grow frustrated when I try to explain something and a student doesn't understand."

However, BIG however, with a deep breath, I have a lot of knowledge and experience with the artistic process that I love to share with others.

I became clearly aware of the difference between the two when I presented workshops about "The 54" in two different formats. The first was a hands on, all in, everyone gets messy with the materials and paints their own painting workshop. They loved it. I went home exhausted.

The other was more of a talk with a demonstration. They listened. I answered questions. We laughed together. I painted a quick demo. It was fun for all. And I was sad to see the time together come to a close. I went home exhilarated.

Lesson learned, for me. I'm not cut out to be an art teacher, at least not right now. I do, however, crave opportunities to share what I've learned about the bigger picture of how to make time to be creative, ways to silence the critics, both internal and external, and practical ways to DO your creative thing.

At one of the speaking engagements I was asked, "what's next?"

Having spent the majority of time the past two years creating small landscape paintings devoid of people, I intend to create a new series of large figurative paintings, celebrating fun times in the sun and water.

I also intend to write what I am calling for now simply "Mimi's Art Book." It will be a book about the creative process, as I have come to know and understand it, to encourage others with practical suggestions for how to explore their own creative gifts.

Here is a small taste of what I mean.

MAKE TIME IN THE MARGINS

I often hear, "if I could only go away on retreat somewhere then I could do it" as an excuse of why someone is not painting/writing/singing/*(fill in the blank with your own creative thing.)*

That sounds delightful, yet for most is unrealistic. My own experience when I've attempted to go away for a couple of days to paint is that I tend to do things like sleep, read, explore, and rarely get much painting done.

Rather, my most successful times when I have needed to restart my painting practice have been when I have set a tiny daily goal. Let's say five minutes a day of sketching. Five minutes. You can find that. Five minutes less scrolling, or talking on the phone. Five minutes committed to your 'thing.'

Here's the basic math. Five minutes a day is 35 minutes a week, or two and a half hours a month. And yes, sometimes that five minutes may turn into a longer time, as your schedule allows. While five minutes may seem to you like too short, and you won't be able to get anything done, you may be surprised to experience what happens when you put your heart, hands, and mind into your creative 'thing' on a daily basis, even in tiny bits of time.

Consider yourself challenged. Close this book. Set the timer on your phone for five minutes. Now go. PLAY!

FOR MY FELLOW CREATIVES

Ok, so now I'm curious! Did you try the five minutes a day I suggested on the previous page? If yes, please consider answering the following five questions.

What is your personal creative indulgence?

How many days did you spend a minimum of five minutes a day with it?

In what way(s) were you pleasantly surprised by the experience?

What did you learn about yourself in the process?

Will you continue now that you've started?

I would love to hear from you! Please share with me by email at mimi@mimisart.com.

Happy creating!

Mimi

Mimi Schlichter is an artist, author, and musician.

She is passionate about faith, family, and friends.

Bio and painting inventory at MimisArt.com

Blog at ArtistsRealLife.com

You may scan the QR code below for direct link to MimisArt.com

Mimi is available to speak to groups and book clubs about her creative process,
either virtually or in person. The painting below is her personal favorite of the hundreds she has created.
It is titled "The Real Me."

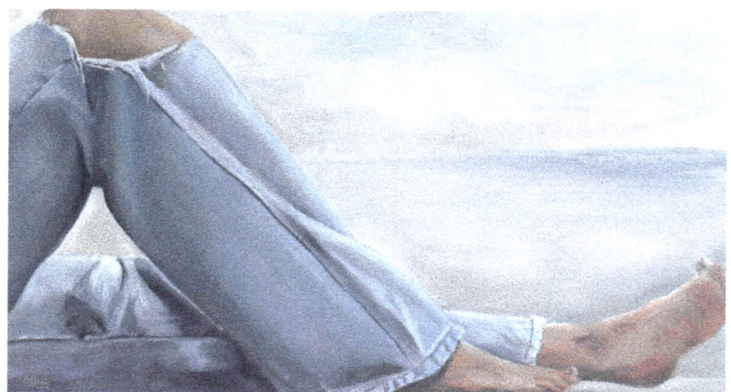